Ordination

A PRACTICAL GUIDE
TO PREPARATION

John 15:16
"Ye have not chosen me, but I have chosen you, and
ordained you, that ye should go and bring forth fruit, and
that your fruit should remain: that whatsoever ye shall
ask of the Father in my name, he may give it you."

Joyce A. Young, B.A., M.S., Ph.D.
Mildred L. Session Meney, B.A., M.S., Ph.D.

WESTBOW
PRESS®
A DIVISION OF THOMAS NELSON
& ZONDERVAN

WestBow Press books may be ordered through booksellers or by contacting:

WestBow Press
A Division of Thomas Nelson & Zondervan
1663 Liberty Drive
Bloomington, IN 47403
www.westbowpress.com
844-714-3454

Scripture taken from the King James Version of the Bible.

ISBN: 978-1-6642-5532-6 (sc)
ISBN: 978-1-6642-5534-0 (hc)
ISBN: 978-1-6642-5533-3 (e)

Library of Congress Control Number: 2022900502

Print information available on the last page.

WestBow Press rev. date: 04/05/2022

CONTENTS

CONTENTS

DR. JOYCE A. YOUNG

Rev. Dr. Joyce A. Young

Dr. Joyce A. Young has been active in the church from an early age. She was baptized at the age of ten and began directing the Youth Choir at Good Hope M.B. Church in Buchanan, Michigan. When her family moved to South Bend, Indiana, she joined Saints Memorial Church of God in Christ where she continued working in the Music Ministry. She later joined Emmanuel Church of God in Christ in South Bend where she served as church secretary, choir director, youth ministry coordinator, and radio broadcast announcer. It was here that she was licensed as an Evangelist.

After graduating from college, she relocated to Rochester, New York, and worked in the Music and Teaching Ministries at Powerhouse Church of God in Christ, Bethesda Church of God in Christ, and later, the Zion Hill Missionary Baptist Church. She had the privilege of organizing and directing a recording choir of over 50 voices known as The Revelation Choir. The choir traveled to correctional facilities throughout the state of New York, and to various locales across the country, opening concerts for many of the nation's top Gospel recording artists, and producing two recordings under her direction.

She was ordained to the Gospel Ministry and Pastorate by the late Apostle Anthony E. Moses of Trinity Fellowship Association (Norfolk, Virginia), who also consecrated her to the esteemed Office of Apostle in 2012. She has served as national secretary of God's End Time Prophetic Revelation Ministries, Inc. (headquarted in Rochester, New York) since 2013. In 2018 she was appointed Assistant National Superior of Women for God's Endtime Prophetic Revelation Ministries, Inc. under the leadership of Chief Apostle S.N. Matthias. She is currently pastor of Triedstone M.B. Church (Rochester, New York).

Pastor Young is a revivalist, workshop presenter and skilled trainer of individuals in the secular world and in ministry. While working at Xerox Corporation, she served on the Adjunct Faculty, training all levels of management in the art of making presentations. She sponsors an annual Women's Empowerment Conference and Fire Conference to encourage, train and equip the people of God to operate in their God-given callings in the spirit of excellence.

Pastor Young earned her B.A. degree from St. Mary's College (Notre Dame, Indiana) and M.S. in Education from Capella University (Minneapolis, Minnesota). She continued her credentialling through the Sacramento Theological Seminary and Bible College, where she was awarded an Honorary Doctor of Divinity degree and the Doctor of Philosophy in Christian Counseling degree. She wrote, directed and performed in the stageplay, "*Stop the World, I Want to Get Off*". She is also the author of a self-published book entitled, "Surviving the Wait," which attempts to encourage individuals waiting for an answer to prayer. As a free-lance writer, Pastor Young has written feature articles for *about ... time* Magazine, a locally-based, nationally circulated magazine.

This Woman of God has a heart for the homeless population and misguided youth. Her vision is to prepare the people of God for the last day harvest and alleviate the suffering of the less fortunate. Her desire is to establish a Christ-centered counseling center that will serve individuals from all walks of life regardless of their ability to pay. Pastor Young is a mother, grandmother, Godmother and mentor to many.

DR. MILDRED L. SESSION MENEY

Rev. Dr. Mildred Session

Dr. Mildred L. Session Meney is well known as a master teacher. She transforms ordinary people into dynamic high achievers. Dr. Session has been a New York State licensed and certified teacher for over thirty-seven years. As a child, she was pastored by the late Reverend Dr. G.G. Gary at Holy City Church of God in Christ (Rochester, New York). As a young adult, she was pastored by Bishop Joseph Lacey at Emmanuel Temple, Pentecostal Assemblies of the World. She was later groomed for pastoral and leadership duties by Bishop Eulah M. Nelson at Bibleway Healing Temple, Pentecostal Assemblies of the World. It was while at Bibleway, that she began hosting and producing her television broadcast, *The Christian Counseling Ministry*, in 1995.

Dr. Session has traveled to numerous cities and locales to mentor, teach and counsel as a Professional Leadership Consultant and Trainer. She is yet a coach and mentor to many pastors, pastors' wives, and their churches. Not only does she train church ministry staff, she was hired as a Professional Development Educational Consultant and Trainer for the YWCA and the New York State Department of Social Services. Because she is well acquainted with the struggles that we often go through in life and having obtained help from God who has sustained her and kept her focused, God has made her a skilled helper who is positioned and able to successfully minister to others. Pastor Session's prophetic voice is called to speak God's blessings, strength, and healing into the lives of his people. She has a sensitive heart for young people, women, and people in leadership. She refers to herself as a "Woman of Purpose with a Purpose." Since 2009, Dr. Session has been hosting her annual "Women of Purpose Conference." During this same time, God birthed in her spirit the establishment of the "Daughters of Lydia." These are women who realize God has a special call on their lives and they choose to answer "YES" to His will. Dr. Session serves as a spiritual mother and mentor to these awesome Women of God.

Dr. Session was consecrated to the Office of Bishop-Elect to the Office of Bishop in August, 2010, and to the esteemed Office of the Apostle, Chief Apostle and Presiding Prelate of Unique Ministries Christian Fellowship International in 2012.

Dr. Mildred Session Meney is founder and pastor of Unique Ministries Church, Inc., in Rochester, NY. With godly insight she served as Vice-President, Women Pastors Empowerment Group. As a leader and a role model, she served as the National Supervisor of Women, God's End Time Prophetic Revelation Ministries, Inc., in Rochester, NY. She enjoys being an Adjunct Professor for the International University of Grace & Truth from which she received her Doctoral degree in Christian Education and Christian Counseling. She is founder and overseer of the ministry training institute, "Kingdom Builders." She continuously writes articles and lesson outlines, and develops a variety of training manuals for corporate leaders and church leaders, alike. Most recently, she pubished her newest training manual entitled, "Equipping Leaders for Ministry in the Spirit of Excellence." Because of the call of God upon her life to build, teach, train, and mentor, God has blessed and allowed her to be Bishop and Overseer to churches in Rochester, NY and Baltimore, MD. Presently, as Dr. Session is challenged to keep moving forward in God, His divine will for her life unfolds in more areas and dimensions than she ever imagined, and her answer still is "Yes, Lord, Yes!" This "Woman of Purpose with a Purpose" is a pastor, mentor, mother, grandmother, and minister of the Gospel with a word of encouragement to share.

PREFACE

Like countless individuals before you, you believe you have been called into the Ministry. The truth of the matter is EVERYONE is called into ministry. To minister is to serve. Jesus gave the clarion call when He issued what we refer to as "The Great Commission" to his disciples in *Matthew 28:19-20*:

"Go ye therefore, and teach all nations, baptizing them in the name of the Father, and of the Son, and of the Holy Ghost: Teaching them to observe all things whatsoever I have commanded you: and, lo, I am with you always, even unto the end of the world."

The difficulty is that far too many individuals who say they have accepted Christ as their savior and are Christians, are not demonstrating the character of a disciple of Christ. Being a disciple means that we follow the teachings, share the thoughts and priorities, have the same passions and goals, and exhibit the character of the one we are following. Many individuals have accepted Christ's redemptive work at Calvary, and that is enough for entry level salvation. Yet, scores of converts have not matured to the point that they have become true disciples. This is because they have not developed the "mindset" of Jesus Christ. That mindset is not something you receive the moment you repeat the sinner's prayer, give the pastor your hand, and join the local church. That mindset is the result of a guided journey by the Holy Spirit, causing you to grow in the grace and knowledge of our Lord and Savior Jesus Christ (*II Peter 3:18*).

Growing in grace is a direct result of your increased knowledge of Christ and the full extent of the work He accomplished for you at Calvary. The more you learn of Him, the greater will be your desire to be like Him. The undeniable evidence that you have developed the mindset of Jesus is your unrelenting "thirst" that He expressed as He cried out from the cross, "I thirst." Humanity believed at the time that He was merely expressing His human need for a drink of water to bring some relief to His suffering. Quite the contrary. Jesus' thirst was for the souls of men He envisioned coming into the Kingdom when His mission was complete. His thirst was the overwhelming, ever-present yearning for the reconciliation of God and man.

I imagine He also longed for the fellowship of His Father, who could no longer bear to look upon Him because He had BECOME the very thing He had so willingly TAKEN UPON Himself ... the totality of man's sin (*II Corinthians 5:21*):

"For he hath made him to be sin for us, who knew no sin; that we might be made the righteousness of God in him."

While on earth, Jesus' mind was always occupied with doing the will of the Father who sent Him. It was His full focus. He clearly expressed this to His disciples as they left Him in search of natural food. Jesus, on the other hand, waited in eager anticipation of His divine appointment with the woman at the well:

"Jesus saith unto them, My meat is to do the will of him that sent me, and to finish his work." John 4:34

The Bible declares that we are to be **IN** the world, but not **OF** the world (*John 1:10*). When we are **OF** the world, we follow the dictates of the world, doing what the world wants, the way the world wants. Our focus follows that of the world with its fads and standards. However, when we have been transformed by the renewing of our minds (*Romans 12:12*) we will have the mind of Christ. This new mind pushes us beyond what the world wants or sees as important. With the mind of Christ, **YOUR** life's agenda becomes **HIS** agenda. What is His agenda? **HIS** agenda is that none should perish, but that everyone will repent (*II Peter 3:9*). **HIS** agenda is total healing for the soul, mind, and body of all mankind.

When **HIS** agenda becomes **YOUR** agenda, you will begin to prepare yourself as an instrument in His hands, fully yielded for His divine purpose. It is at that point you begin to live your life on purpose. If **HIS** agenda is not yet **YOUR** agenda, you are not yet ready for this journey.

God had (and yet has) plans specific to you. His message to the prophet Jeremiah applies to you and should inspire you:

"For I know the thoughts that I think toward you, saith the LORD, *thoughts of peace, and not of evil, to give you an expected end"* (*Jeremiah 29:11*).

Read the statement God makes to the prophet in *Jeremiah 1:5*:

"Before I formed thee in the belly I knew thee; and before thou camest forth out of the womb I sanctified thee, and I ordained thee a prophet unto the nations."

Just as in the prophet's case, God knew every road you would wander down and every corner you would turn. So, He began preparing you for your spiritual destiny from the moment you were conceived.

God knew what attributes you needed for the unique design He had in mind for you. Have you ever thought how special you must be to God? He has painstakingly and lovingly invested time and energy into you, watching over every aspect of your development from your conception to the present moment. He worked behind the scenes to get you to the point you are today, fully accepting your call to Ministry, investing your time, and denying yourself to partner with Him in your own spiritual development. Think of it! You now **work in partnership with the Spirit of God on this journey.**

You are on the road to ordination, a major phase in being presented to the world as a fully equipped and acceptable Minister of the Gospel. As you enter this phase of preparation, do so prayerfully, reverently, and with great expectation of a higher level of servitude than ever before. You should also expect and prepare yourself for new spiritual challenges because of the stand you are now called to take. Some of the challenges may manifest as problems in the natural. Many of them, however, are spiritual in nature. Weapons will form against you that you had no idea even existed. Weapons will form against you that you did not believe could be invented! The good news is, however, that you have this promise on the greatest authority (the Word of God): *"No weapon formed against you shall prosper ..."* (*Isaiah 54:17*). You should be both excited and humbled by the opportunity to officially become a member of the special task force known as **The Kingdom Builders on Earth**.

This booklet is designed to give you some fundamentals to help you develop your personal perspective and increase your knowledge base, so you are equipped to fight the good fight of faith in an ever-changing world.

INTRODUCTION

ORDINATION is the process by which your local church publicly and officially attests to your being prepared to assume a broader range of ministerial responsibilities. In many denominations, it is the right of the local church to determine the policies and procedures surrounding licensure and ordination of its ministers. This also includes the qualifications of those individuals who may be licensed and/or ordained. If the local church is part of a broader association of churches, it may choose to coordinate the process with the association. Independent churches may also elect to coordinate this process with churches of similar beliefs and doctrine with whom they fellowship.

It is also within the authority of your local church to evaluate your commitment to the call, and whether you are pursuing it in the spirit of excellence. Of major concern is your spiritual development. It is not expected that you be "perfect" in terms of comportment or fully knowledgeable in all matters pertaining to ministry operation and duties as you begin your road to ordination. It **IS** expected, however, that you can be viewed as an example and a "life model" for others ... one who is clearly striving to emulate the character of Christ. Lay members and newer ministers should be able to look upon you as one to follow as you follow Christ. It is also expected that you are clearly committed to upward mobility and growing in the ways that please God. As a candidate for ordination, these terms should describe you as you advance in knowledge and proficiency in the Word. Your total dependence upon God in every area of your life (natural and spiritual) should be abundantly clear. The Apostle Paul describes it as pressing *"toward the mark for the prize of the high calling of God in Christ Jesus"* (*Philippians 3:14*).

The local church's responsibility (or in some cases, the association's or denomination's) is to set any training, counseling, and monitoring requirements necessary to prepare you, the candidate, for the ordination process. Your life will now become similar to that of any politician ... an open book, subjected to ever increasing scrutiny. Your church leadership will provide oversight to ensure your continued adherence to the biblical principles and church doctrine that are necessary for effective ministry. It is incumbent upon the local church to spare no effort to assist you in meeting the standards of faithfulness, commitment, personal attributes, knowledge acquisition, and the skill sets vital to ministry in contemporary society.

A majority of churches today believe that all Christians are ministers at a very basic level, called to be witnesses of the change Christ has brought to their personal lives. This witnessing is aimed at bringing souls to repentance and to an acceptance of Christ as Lord and Savior. As such, the born-again believer becomes a part of the "priesthood" of Christ. This is also demonstrated by water baptism in which the convert shares in the burial and resurrection of Jesus Christ. This act of obedience is a testimony to the world that the new convert has taken on the nature of Christ and has forsaken the things of the world. Shared by most churches, this belief is incorporated into their doctrines. That said, ordination is the church's public affirmation of your call to this vocation and of your having fully complied with the Ordinances and doctrine of the Church.

In the early church, the highlight of the ordination service was the "laying on of hands." This was also evidence of the church's belief the individual had been called of God and dedicated to His service. By the laying on of their hands, the early Apostles authorized the new ministers to also serve on their behalf (*Acts 6:6 and 13:3; 1 Timothy 4:14; 2 Timothy 1:6*). Thus, the laying on of hands also represented a literal and direct transfer of power and authority to share in the work of the ministry. Reflect for a moment on the implications of this fact, which continues to be a central theme in Ordination Services. Today, the act of laying on of hands, anointing with oil and offering prayer for the candidate, are focal points in any ministerial installation service or service of elevation. Together, these acts bring together in **ONE** person, the ministry of **MANY** persons who themselves, are representatives of the Body of Christ. Recognizing this, godly wisdom must be exercised on the part of the local church in selecting the individuals who will have the **PRIVILEGE** of participating in the "laying on of hands."

Remind yourself often that pursuing ordination is actively seeking to advance to greater self-sacrifice. It is not the all-too-often mistaken "road to glory and fame" that many envision. This journey you are undertaking is a lonely one, scattered with pitfalls, potholes, hurdles, speed bumps, and some detours. This journey takes away your sense of having a life of your own. You will no longer belong to yourself. You will have no life except the life you live in and through Christ Jesus.

There will be times you will say, *"I didn't sign up for this,"* or *"Somebody forgot to send me the memo on this one."* Despite those feelings and the temptation to back down, step aside or relinquish your position, the act of turning back will not be an option. This life may have some "thankless" moments, as well. The suffering you endure for the sake of the ministry entrusted to you cannot be compared to what God has reserved just for you. This life of dedication and sacrifice will be rewarding beyond your imagination, both in this world and the world to come. The fringe benefits have no comparison to any recognition or compensation the world has to offer you. Recognizing the hour on the spiritual time clock, we all must realize it is time to proceed with all diligence in pursuit of *"the prize for the high calling of God in Christ Jesus"* (*Philippians 3:14*).

PART I

—

A DIVINE ASSIGNMENT

THE SIGNIFICANCE OF ORDINATION

Ordination in any church is a matter of tremendous importance. This event places you at a totally different level in terms of how you are viewed by those around you. You will be under closer scrutiny by those closest to you. Those you thought would never judge you, nor leave you, may begin doing just that ... judging you and ultimately walking away from you because they see you as having "changed." Indeed, you will have changed to conform to the nature of Christ. As you walk more in the light, it becomes more difficult to fellowship with the darkness around you. Therefore, do not be alarmed if acquaintances become fewer as you are elevated.

With ordination comes far greater responsibilities than you have had previously, or that you may even have thought of having. What you do and how you perform in ministry will have a more dramatic and lasting effect on the lives of God's people ... His sheep who must be led, protected and fed. You have a Divine Assignment, and you are now preparing yourself to step fully into that assignment. You must always remember that this assignment was not given to you by man. Despite that fact, you will have to answer to human leadership, but ultimately to God Himself.

Through the process of ordination, man merely **CONFIRMS** what God has **PREDESTINED**. Therefore, it must not be taken lightly, but approached with all gravity. As an ordained minister or deacon, you are publicly and unreservedly responding to the Savior's mandate in The Great Commission (*Matthew 28:19*). That mandate focuses on meeting the needs of the people of God at your local church and beyond. You may not agree with some of the individuals you will be serving, and some may even be a challenge to love. Nevertheless, you must serve them **and love them** with the **unconditional love of the Lord**.

Occasions (though they should be rare) may arise when you may even find yourself lacking full agreement with your leadership. How will you handle such situations? The scripture admonishes us in *Hebrews 13:17* to: "*Obey them that have the rule over you and submit yourselves: for they watch for your souls, as they that must give account, that they may do it with joy, and not with grief: for that* is *unprofitable for you.*" You are to be loyal, faithful, and obedient. This will only be achieved as you view them through God's eyes. God looks upon each person, regardless of his/her position, as a precious son or daughter with a soul to be saved, delivered, guided to his/her destiny, and prepared to live eternally with Him. Your leaders are gifted, and they are chosen of God; however, they are human. This simply means that, despite their gifts and callings, they yet have the propensity to err. As the person in the mirror, remember that you have the same propensity for error.

Once ordained, you will be identified by members of your local church and the community as an official representative of your church. This means that wherever you are, in town or out of town, at home or downtown, in the church edifice or at your place of employment, at the grocery store or in the mall, you always represent three entities. These entities consist of your local church, your pastor, and above all, your Heavenly Father. Knowing that, your comportment must always be of the highest standard, consistently reflecting the nature of Christ. You can allow no individual or situation to cause you to step out of your character. Your temperament and disposition will always be on display, and they must always be predictable and appropriate. Although your old man is yet present, he must remain in constant submission to the new man. When you encounter any challenge, ask yourself the question, "What would Jesus do?" and then DO THAT! You do not want to jeopardize the effective and successful completion of your assignment by a "false step," or error in judgement.

Upon ordination, certain expectations are a given. There may have been occasions prior to ordination when you were not as faithful to services or church events as you could have been. Perhaps you were not as dutiful in your giving or stepping up to assume leadership roles as you should have been. Because you only held a license, your absence or failure to "lead" was not as critically looked upon as it will be at this new level. You will now be looked up to as an assistant to the pastor and governing board that leads the church.

In your new capacity, you are in effect, the pastor's right hand, deemed capable of helping to carry the weight of the ministry. In fact, you are being strategically placed for that very purpose. You are not merely adding a title to your name. You are **CONSCIOUSLY AND OPENLY DECIDING TO ACCEPT YOUR SHARE OF A BURDEN.** The burden is indeed a heavy one, for it consists of all the disappointments, frustrations, illnesses, fears, heartaches, failures, apprehensions, sorrows and yes, even the successes of each member of the congregation. You must own a piece of every challenge that arises through the operation of the ministry. This is not a position of power or honor you have aspired to. Rather, it relegates you to the lowest position. You are emphatically stating you are taking the ministry upon your shoulders. This shows your willingness to lift, carry and build a ministry that has the capacity to fulfill the mission, vision, and the plan of God for the local church, and the local church's position in the universal church, as well. You are, in effect, becoming a vital part of a much larger vision.

If you are a "driven" person who likes to see things move forward quickly, you may be disappointed many times along your journey. You cannot simply decide to take a break or quit when things do not go as you think they should. You cannot afford to be seen as "throwing in the towel" when unexpected challenges arise. Congregants will look to you as an example to follow, **SO LEAD.** You must never forget the influence your actions have on members of the congregation, the quality and effectiveness of the ministry, and the ministry's reputation in the community.

Once ordained, your ordination is typically honored for life wherever you go. Keep in mind, however, that should you decide to change denominations or religious associations, you may encounter leadership that requires additional training and/or ordination procedures other than those you already possess.

THE IMAGE IN THE MIRROR

Man looking in the mirror

Few people can get dressed without the aid of a mirror. Called a looking glass by some, a mirror is an object that reflects light. It does so in such a way that the reflected light preserves most of the physical details of the original light. The result is your ability to see your physical appearance as others will see it. For many, it will be necessary to return to the mirror to "check things out" several times prior to leaving the house, and perhaps even make some adjustments. Most prefer a full-length mirror to judge their total appearance. This allows them to ensure that everything is *in place and in order*. Your spiritual mirror experience will be no different.

It is vital that each servant of God look in the mirror and "check out" his/her spiritual appearance. This is essential because the One we want to please is God, and the only way to achieve that, is to reflect His image. Ministry at any level will prove ineffective if this is not the case. The mirror utilized for this purpose is of course, The Bible, God's Word, His blueprint for mankind. There is no more desirable time than now to return to the mirror and engage in some introspection. As you do so, questions should come to mind.

The questions you, as a candidate for ordination, should be asking yourself before reading any further in this preparation guide or pursuing the path to ordination, are:

❖ "Am I certain God is pleased with my life?"
   (NOTE: The question is NOT: "Is my life perfectly lined up with the Word of God?")

❖ "Am I certain I have been called to this specialized area of ministry?"

❖ "Who am I in God?"

❖ "What is my motive for seeking ordination?"

❖ "Am I ready to make the sacrifices that ordination requires?"

❖ "What are my gifts and talents?"

❖ "What are my areas of challenge?"

❖ Ministers: "Which of the Five-Fold Ministry Offices am I called to?"

❖ Deacons: "How do I know I am called to the Office of the Deacon?"

If you are having difficulty answering the above questions, you may close this book now and return it to your pastor with your regrets. Or, you may elect to proceed, admitting to yourself first, and then to God (Who already knows everything there is to know about you, anyway), that you cannot truthfully answer all of them at this moment. Perhaps you realize, however, that you are a "work in progress within a process". Are you willing to fully give yourself to that process? Are you dedicated to the fulfillment of your destiny? Are you committed to pleasing the One Who has given you everything and withheld nothing?

If your response to these questions is "Yes", rest assured this journey will require extraordinary commitment. The enemy of your soul is certainly not going to simply go away, sit down, cross his legs, fold his arms, and admit defeat. Rather, the enemy will make every effort to distract you, show you short cuts (which, by the way, will only result in delaying your success). He will even tempt you to avoid some of the learning opportunities you may find challenging or uncomfortable. If you persevere, however, you will be prepared to meet the challenges of ministry and show yourself to be a workman that needs to feel no shame as you serve God's people. You will be a veritable agent of change because as you behold yourself in God's mirror, what will be reflected, will be the character of God.

Woman with hands up

As you increase and deepen your level of introspection, you will become painfully aware of your short-comings and total dependence upon God. The result is total surrender to a flawless God with a perfect plan for your life.

RE-EVALUATING YOUR MOTIVATION

Your motive for advancing in ministry should be synonymous with the reasons God gave the Five-Fold Ministry Offices to the church. These Offices are often referred to as "The Ascension Gifts" since Jesus instituted them just prior to His ascension. The Five-Fold Ministry and its purpose is listed in *Ephesians 4:11-16*:

"And he gave some, apostles; and some, prophets; and some, evangelists; and some, pastors and teachers; For the perfecting of the saints, for the work of the ministry, for the edifying of the body of Christ: Till we all come in the unity of the faith, and of the knowledge of the Son of God, unto a perfect man, unto the measure of the stature of the fulness of Christ: That we henceforth be no more children, tossed to and fro, and carried about with every wind of doctrine, by the sleight of men, and cunning craftiness, whereby they lie in wait to deceive; But speaking the truth in love, may grow up into him in all things, which is the head, even Christ: From whom the whole body fitly joined together and compacted by that which every joint supplieth, according to the effectual working in the measure of every part, maketh increase of the body unto the edifying of itself in love."

The Apostle Paul's vision and statement of the purpose for these gift offices should serve as your motivation in pursuing a higher level in ministry. You should long for what the Apostle Paul saw:

- The church becoming united in faith and in the knowledge of Jesus Christ
- The church coming to maturity in Christ
- The church no longer being deceived and led astray by false teachings, but rather being stable, consistent, effective, and efficient
- The church thriving because the ministry is working as God designed it to work; all ministers faithfully and effectively working in the capacities to which they are called.

Your responsibility is to discover your position in the Five-Fold Ministry, accept it, and occupy that position through the power of the Holy Spirit. Given the spiritual climate in contemporary society, none of us has the luxury of offering ministry with anything less than the spirit of excellence.

If any ministry is to mature and succeed, the individual members of that ministry must, of necessity, be mature. This means effectively utilizing their gifts and callings for the glory of God. The subjects of spiritual gifts and spiritual maturity are covered more extensively in Part II.

PART II

—

PREPARING FOR ORDAINED MINISTRY

PRE-REQUISITES FOR ORDINATION

Each denomination has its own standards which potential leaders are expected to meet when being considered for ordination. Nearly all denominations require some degree of formal educational achievements (Bible College or seminary training). Training may also be required through the local church, followed by licensure by the local church or the affiliated church organization. Licensure usually takes place soon after the individual has:

1. Publicly acknowledged his/her call to the pulpit ministry
2. Demonstrated his/her knowledge of scripture
3. Demonstrated a commitment to the Christian life and to the local church
4. Sufficiently demonstrated his/her ability to prepare and deliver a sermon

The latter is often accomplished through what is referred to as a "Trial Sermon" or "Inaugural Sermon." In many churches, a special service is held to afford the prospective minister the opportunity to demonstrate his/her ability to deliver a sermon. The individual is then granted a "License" at this service. This license officially provides the individual the right and charge to continue developing his/her ministerial skills through increased study and involvement in any and all activities that will promote spiritual growth. It is understood that the individual's growth and development will be evaluated periodically by the local pastor. Thus begins the road to ordination.

Candidates may receive training through a seminary and/or training through the local church. At a minimum, the training should focus on various aspects of ministry, including, but not limited to:

- A Survey of Biblical History
- Understanding the Unifying Theme of the Bible
- Surveying the Old and New Testaments
- Church Administration
- Sermon Preparation
- Elements of Worship (Administering the Sacraments, Conducting Worship Services)
- Ministry Events (Weddings, Funerals, Pastoral Counseling, Baptisms and Baby Christenings)
- The Importance of Missions
- Servant Leadership
- Pastoral Counseling
- Character Development
- Discovering and Developing Spiritual Gifts

The requirements for licensing and ordination vary widely. This is particularly true in churches that are independent of a larger governing body which would guide those processes. Most churches do, however, adhere to guidelines for licensing and ordination that are generally accepted and followed by other churches.

Once the licensed minister has met all the conditions set forth by the local church, he/she is eligible to proceed toward ordination. Although we all become witnesses at conversion, ordination prepares the candidate for a more specific area of ministry. Because of this, the basic denominational prerequisites for ordination include adherence to biblical mandates. The following is a generally accepted prerequisite checklist:

The candidate for ordination must have:

- openly and boldly confessed Christ as his/her personal savior
- been a faithful, active member of the local church for a minimum of one year
- demonstrated loyalty and commitment to the local church and its leadership
- demonstrated a teachable spirit
- demonstrated the ability to follow through with assignments from leadership
- exhibited the character of Christ
- demonstrated the self-discipline necessary for leadership
- modeled leadership skills
- shown a love for the Word of God
- shown an uncommon love for the people of God and a desire to lead them to their divine destiny
- demonstrated the ability to "rightly divide the Word of Truth"
- modeled the Fruit of the Spirit through his/her words and deeds
- acknowledged an awareness of the Gifts of the Spirit in his/her life
- openly and boldly confessed his/her calling to serve in the Gospel ministry
- been licensed in the local church for a time specified by the pastor, usually not less than 2 years. This timeframe is for training and development and may vary from person to person, and ministry to ministry, at the discretion of the pastor, or as dictated by local church policy.
- acknowledged adherence to the Bible as the infallible, inerrant, and inspired Word of God.

BIBLICAL QUALIFICATIONS FOR ORDAINED MINISTRY

As human beings who prefer not to experience discomfort in our flesh, we are often tempted to complain about things that happen to us in our lifetimes. Whenever challenges confront us, we ask ourselves, "Why me?" We may even compare ourselves to someone else who is not experiencing hurdles as high as our own. The truth is, everything that comes our way is specifically for us, and it is for our benefit. (See *Romans 8:28*).

God knows us so well that He is aware of what will be necessary to lead us through the developmental stages to the Christ-like character He desires to see in us. Who we are when no one is looking and what we do in our personal lives in terms of habits and everyday conduct, affect our aptitude **FOR** ministry and our altitude **IN** ministry.

The Apostle Paul was a no-nonsense person prior to his conversion on the road to Damascus. He was fully committed to his job of persecuting the early church. Following his conversion, he demonstrated the same zeal in building up the church as he previously demonstrated in trying to destroy the church. He simply re-directed his sense of dedication. Consistent with his whole-hearted approach to his vocation, he provided his son in the ministry, the young Timothy, with some very stringent characteristics for people in ministry.

Ministerial Qualifications According to The Apostle Paul:

In *I Timothy 3*, and *Titus 1*, the Apostle Paul addresses the "Qualifications of Church Officers" in terms of character, conduct and effectiveness in ministry. If your personal life and conduct are not in line with the Word of God, your ministering will be ineffective from the Pulpit. Let us review the list of characteristics as presented by the Apostle Paul:

1. Blameless
2. Husband of one wife
3. Vigilant
4. Sober
5. Of good behavior
6. Given to hospitality
7. Apt to teach
8. Not a drinker
9. No striker (argumentative individual)
10. Not greedy of filthy lucre
11. Patient
12. Not a brawler
13. Not covetous
14. In control of his own house
15. Having obedient and respectful children
16. Not a novice (without experience)
17. Good reputation in his community
18. Serious-minded
19. Truthful
20. Holding the secrets of the faith with a clear conscience

> As you compare these qualifications to your own life, you may initially feel the bar is set too high. However, surrender to a forgiving and empowering God, makes those standards attainable.

All the above qualifications presented by the Apostle Paul describe the character traits that should be evident in effective ministers of the Gospel. They were of such significance that he spent considerable time and energy outlining them. This is because he understood that the degree to which God would be able to use an individual is contingent upon that person's character.

Notice that in *I Timothy, chapter 4,* the Apostle Paul continues this theme. He instructs Timothy to remind the brethren of some additional key concepts that are essential for effective ministry. The brethren must:

- Be good ministers of Jesus Christ, nourished up in the words of faith … (*vs. 6-11*)
- Be examples of the believers in word, in conversation, in charity, in spirit, in faith (*v. 12*)
- Give attention to spending time in the Word of God, exhortation, and to doctrine (*vs. 13-16*)
- Pay attention to their God-given gifts
- Focus on themselves, giving sincere attention to continuing in the doctrine
- Respect the elders, rather than rebuking them, looking upon them as fathers (*1 Timothy 5:1-2*).

Your character is foundational to your motivation behind advancing in ministry. Individuals seek to enter or advance within the ministry for a myriad of reasons. Remember this key point: as a minister of the Gospel of Jesus Christ, you are to always seek to not only represent but to **PROMOTE Christ**. He must **ALWAYS** be the One on display. If what you do puts **YOU** on display, the **WRONG person is being seen**. Using your calling and giftings for any other reason is an affront to the Word of God and to God Himself.

You will be prompted on several occasions throughout this guide to re-evaluate your motivation for beginning this journey.

THE FRUIT OF THE SPIRIT

"But the fruit of the Spirit is love, joy, peace, longsuffering, kindness, goodness, faithfulness, gentleness and self-control. Against such things there is no law." (Galatians 5:22-23)

You are certain to have had exhaustive studies on the Fruit of the Spirit during your years of ministry. Why mention the Fruit of the Spirit at this juncture in your ministry? The answer is simple. As a minister of the Word and a leader in the church, you must not only **BE FAMILIAR** with the Fruit of the Spirit, but you must also be **CERTAIN** you possess the fruit, recognize its influence **UPON** your life, and be aware of its manifestation **THROUGH** your life. This is so that anyone you encounter can see it so clearly that it is as if you are wearing a sign around your neck announcing: "I exude the Fruit of the Spirit." The Greek word translated "fruit" refers to the natural product of a living thing. Paul used "fruit" to help us understand the attributes produced by the Holy Spirit, who lives inside every believer. You cannot produce the Fruit, no matter how hard you may try. The Fruit of the Spirit can only be produced by the Spirit Himself, for the Fruit is the character of the Spirit. Notice, the Greek word for fruit is singular, not the plural "fruits" as many mistakenly say. By using the singular form of the word "fruit" helps us to understand these character traits are not independent of one another. Instead, they consist of a unified whole.

As you mature in The Word, all the characteristics of Christ will manifest themselves in and through you. You will be powerless to **STOP** that from happening. Nor can you force it **TO** happen. Simply allow the Spirit to have free course in your life, and He will make Himself known. Just as natural fruit needs time to grow, the Fruit of the Spirit will not ripen in our lives overnight. In the natural, farmers wage never-ending battles against weeds and pests to prevent them from destroying their crops. You, too, must constantly work to rid your life of the old sin nature so it will not choke out the work of Holy Spirit in your life. The power to resist and reject old sinful desires comes from the Holy Spirit. With every temptation, God provides a way (sometimes more than one way) of escape. It is up to you to say "no!" and utilize the "way out" God has provided (*I Corinthians 10:13*). The Holy Spirit leads the way.

As you increasingly give the Holy Spirit control of your life, He begins to do in and through you what only He can do, and that is to mold and shape you into the image of Christ (*II Corinthians 3:17-18*). Since God's goal and desire for all His children is that we be like His Son (*Romans 8:29*), the Holy Spirit constantly works to rid your life of the *"acts of the sinful nature"* (*Galatians 5:19*) so you may display *His* fruit instead. Therefore, the "Fruit of the Spirit" manifested in your life is proof that your character is becoming more like Christ's. You are developing the mindset of Christ. You should be increasingly aware of the Spirit operating in your life daily. No one should have difficulty seeing the Fruit on display. Whenever you interact with others, two things should be abundantly clear. First, people should readily see that there is something genuinely different about you. The second thing people should realize is that this difference comes from an inner place that cannot be disturbed by external forces or circumstances.

The Apostle Paul presents nine fruit (results or evidences) of the Spirit's presence in a person's life. Refer to *Galatians 5:22-23*. They are:

Love

Most in contemporary society see love as much more than a mere emotion. Instead, it is considered a verb ... an action word. Admittedly, you will encounter some individuals in your lifetime and ministry who are a challenge to love. When someone has been filled with the Holy Spirit, however, loving others becomes second nature. When the Holy Spirit enters, He brings love with Him. He is one with God and the Son, and the Bible declares that God is Love: "*He that loveth not knoweth not God; for God is love*" (*I John 4:8*). Emanating from the believer's character, love causes us to think of the welfare of others before our own. Prior to engaging in a particular behavior, love will prompt us to stop and consider whether the behavior will cause harm or create a stumbling block in the life of a less mature believer. The behavior may be perfectly innocent, and well within the believer's right, but the more mature believer will give up that right out of love (*Romans 14:1-15*). This is what the Apostle Paul meant in *I Corinthians 10:23*: "*All things are lawful, but all things are not expedient: all things are lawful for me, but all things edify not.*" This is crucial because one of the major responsibilities of the minister is to build others up (edify).

Joy

Joy is defined as a feeling of gladness or delight. The world's joy, however, (often used interchangeably with happiness) cannot last because it is based on unstable, natural, temporal surroundings and circumstances. The joy of the Lord, on the other hand, has no basis in what is occurring around us. Our joy has its foundation in a spiritual destiny that is eternal. As we remain in God's presence, we experience the fullness of joy described in *Psalm 16:11*: "*Thou wilt shew me the path of life: in thy presence is fulness of joy; at thy right hand there are pleasures for evermore.*"

That joy then becomes our source of strength (*Nehemiah 8:10*) during times of extreme challenge and testing, when we are tempted to doubt or throw in the towel. Stronger than any circumstances we face, the joy of the Lord lifts us above the challenges and testing, causing us to emerge victoriously.

Peace

Contemporary society has little to offer in terms of peace. Clearly, if the world was acquainted with the Prince of Peace, it would know peace. He declared: *"Peace I leave with you, my peace I give unto you: not as the world giveth, give I unto you. Let not your heart be troubled, neither let it be afraid"* (*John 14:27*). For those who have the Holy Spirit, peace is not a far-fetched dream. It is not merely a possibility for every believer, it is a guarantee. This is because the Holy Spirit brings this unexplainable peace with Him when He takes up residence inside each of us.

If the peace of God is to be fully manifested in our lives, it is imperative that two things happen. First, we must **KNOW** God, not just **KNOW OF** God. Knowing Him is the reward of spending time in His presence, studying His Word, and enduring tests and trials with Him. Secondly, we must surrender all of our concerns to Him, as in *I Peter 5:7: "Casting all your care upon him; for he careth for you."* We must also focus our minds on the things of God as in *Philippians 4:8: "Finally, brethren, whatsoever things are true, whatsoever things are honest, whatsoever things are just, whatsoever things are pure, whatsoever things are lovely, whatsoever things are of good report; if there be any virtue, and if there be any praise, think on these things."*

Longsuffering

Longsuffering (another term for patience) is critically lacking in society today, even in the church world. We live in a microwave, must-have-it-now society. It is rare to find individuals who are willing to embrace "delayed gratification." The growing mentality is "I want what I want, I want it now, and I want it just like I want it." Increasingly few individuals are willing to trust the process of advancement or walk the path to reach a lofty goal. It is with the same attitude that we approach the blessings of God or advancement in the realm of ministry. Christians must exercise longsuffering through the power of the Holy Spirit living within. As Spirit-filled believers, we are gracefully able to endure the most challenging of people and circumstances. *"But they that wait upon the LORD shall renew their strength; they shall mount up with wings as* eagles; *they shall run, and not be weary;* and *they shall walk, and not faint*" (*Isaiah 40:31*).

Gentleness

The individual modeling the attribute of gentleness tends to be a kind, tender, mild-mannered and courteous person. As such, this person is easily entreated, and responds to others with respect and dignity, even in situations when he/she may well be justified (in the world's eyes) in treating someone else in less than a respectful manner: "*Walk in wisdom toward them that are without, redeeming the time. Let your speech be always with grace, seasoned with salt, that ye may know how ye ought to answer every man*" (*Colossians 4:5-6*).

Goodness

Goodness can be thought of as a type of virtue. The individual modeling goodness will demonstrate good moral standards. This trait, along with gentleness, has everything to do with how an individual presents him/herself to others. Not only do they speak to how you interact with others, but they also influence how effective you will be in those interactions.

Faith

Faith is fundamental to Christianity. It is such an essential trait that it is mentioned 336 times in the King James Version of the Holy Bible. We are "*saved by grace through faith*" (*Ephesians 2:8*). We also know that it takes faith to please God (*Hebrews 11:6*), and rather than living our lives by what we can see, "*we walk by faith*" (*II Corinthians 5:7*). For the Christian, therefore, faith is a way of life.

Our faith, then, results naturally in our faithfulness, which is reliability and trustworthiness. We can be relied upon by God to be loyal to His Word, loyal to His way, and obedient to His commands. By the same token, we can be trusted by our fellow brothers and sisters to live according to godly standards, and to support them through godly counsel and prayer. This also means we can be relied upon to play a meaningful role in the work of the ministry despite enduring persecution *"So that we ourselves glory in you in the churches of God for your patience and faith in all your persecutions and tribulations that ye endure."* (*II Thessalonians 1:4*).

Meekness

Individuals who present themselves as meek are often seen by carnal individuals as weak. This is far from the truth. Meekness is in all actuality, great strength under the strictest degree of control. In the Apostle Paul's second letter to Timothy, he wrote that when we find ourselves in a position to correct others, we should do so with meekness (*II Timothy 2:25*). In his letter to the church in Galatia, he wrote that anyone who had been caught committing sin should not only be restored, but restoration must be accomplished in a certain manner. *"Brethren, if a man be overtaken in a fault, ye which are spiritual, restore such an one in the spirit of meekness; considering thyself, lest thou also be tempted"* (*Galatians 6:1*). To do otherwise undermines unity within the Body of Christ, in addition to the restorer running the risk of falling into the same snare.

Temperance

The last characteristic in the Apostle Paul's Fruit of the Spirit list is temperance, or self-control. The converted child of God exercises control over sinful desires because of the power invested in him/her by the indwelling Holy Spirit. The believer **CAN** say **NO** to the flesh and **YES** to the Spirit of God. The result is spiritual development and a great harvest of souls. This fruit is in direct opposition to the works of the flesh that the Apostle speaks of in *Galatians 5:19-21*.

THE GIFTS OF THE SPIRIT CATEGORIZED

I n *I Corinthians 12:8-12*, the Apostle Paul introduces us to the Gifts of the Holy Spirit, different from the Fruit of the Spirit, and different from each other in meaning and in purpose. Yet, the gifts are all distributed by the Holy Spirit. *"But all these worketh that one and the selfsame Spirit, dividing to every man severally as he will." (v. 11)*. No two gifts are the same, and generally no two believers have the exact same gift. In every instance, however, these gifts are given for the edification, growth, and perfection of the church.

As in any natural gift, these spiritual gifts come without price. Every believer has one or more of these gifts, and it is each believer's responsibility to discover what our gifts are, dedicate them back to God Who gave them, perfect them, and allow ourselves to be used in these gifts to the glory of God.

The Gifts of the Spirit may be sorted according to three major categories:

➢ Revelation Gifts
➢ Power Gift
➢ Speaking Gifts

The Gifts of the Spirit, as presented by the Apostle Paul, along with their categories are:

The Gift of Wisdom (Category: Revelation Gift)

The first gift Paul mentions is the gift of wisdom. It is listed first perhaps because it is foundational to the church. It is also a gift that the believer can earnestly desire. Wisdom is presented in The Word of God as *"The fear of the LORD is the beginning of wisdom; all who follow his precepts have good understanding"* (Psalm 111:10). In *Proverbs 4:7* The Word declares: *"Wisdom is the principal thing; therefore get wisdom: and with all thy getting get understanding."* King Solomon could have asked for any gift from God; yet, the gift he requested and was granted, was the wisdom to rule God's people justly (*I Kings 3:12*). If you could ask God for anything at all, what would it be? Would you lay a noble request before Him and ask Him for more gifting to bless His people in a greater way than before?

The Gift of Knowledge (Category: Revelation Gift)

Have you ever noticed how some people seem to have the natural ability for exceptional recall? Perhaps they have an unusual knowledge of God and the spirit realm. They can quickly distinguish what is biblical and what is not. Perhaps they "just know" when to say something and when to hold their peace. Some translations refer to this gift as the "Word" of Knowledge, while others say that it is the "Utterance" of Knowledge. All these terms are correct. Whichever you choose to call this gift, it is essential to understand that it comes from God, and that it is for the benefit of the believer.

The Gift of Faith (Category: Power Gift)

The next gift the Apostle Paul mentions is the gift of faith. Those with this gift have a unique way of seeing things. Confidence and assurance seem to flow out of them even in the face of the severest challenges. This is because these individuals see circumstances through the eyes of God. He sees things not as they appear to the human eye and looks beyond what the physical reflects. He then issues a command that quickens the potential beyond the physical manifestation and calls into being what does not yet exist outside of the spirit realm: *"As it is written, I have made thee a father of many nations, before him whom he believed, even God, who quickeneth the dead, and calleth those things which be not as though they were" (Romans 4:17).*

The Gifts of Healing (Category: Power Gift)

The gift of healing has been a source of controversy throughout the history of the church. This gift was more prominent in the New Testament Church. It was proof that there was power in the name of Jesus Christ and that God was working in the church. Any healing that took place was attributed to the Holy Spirit and not to man. Men are merely the instruments that God uses to accomplish His will in the earth. Take care that the glory of all that God does through you is accredited to Him.

The Gift of Miracles (Category: Power Gift)

A miracle is an occurrence that cannot be explained by human intervention or scientific reasoning. The gift of working miracles is another gift of the Spirit. These occurrences are always credited to the Spirit and not to human beings. Prayer Warriors and Intercessors are often those who see miraculous answers to their effectual, fervent prayers (*James 5:16*).

The Gift of Prophecy (Category: Speaking Gift)

Prophecy has different meanings throughout the Bible. One of them is teaching or speaking The Word of God. Yet another means to foretell. This use of the term refers to someone supernaturally foretelling events that will come to pass in someone's life or in the life of the church.

Many individuals "flow" in the prophetic realm, but that does not mean those persons walk in the Office of the Prophet. The Holy Spirit can reveal things to a yielded, anointed servant of God, enabling him/her to effectively minister in the prophetic realm at that time.

Other individuals may be influenced by the prophetic atmosphere and may begin to speak prophetically. Such was the case with Saul (*I Samuel 10:10*) when he met the company of prophets. Although he prophesied at that time, Saul was not a prophet.

The Gift of Discernment (Category: Revelation Gift)

Discernment is one gift that every believer is expected to have, if indeed the Spirt of God lives within. This gift automatically comes with the indwelling of the Holy Spirit, empowering the believer to determine which spirits are of God and which are not, when a person is sincere and when he is not, when God is working and when He is not, and to give guidance and advice to the church regarding perspective actions. It is also used to correctly break down the meaning of scripture.

The Apostle Peter demonstrated this gift (*Acts 5:1-10*). Ananias and his wife, Sapphira, sold some of their property to donate to the work of the ministry. Rather than giving the entire profit from the sale to the ministry, they kept a portion for themselves and lied to the Apostle Peter about the amount of the sale. (*Acts 5:1-10*). If your gift of discernment is weak, ask God to sharpen it.

The Gift of Diverse Tongues (Category: Speaking Gift)

The next gift is the ability to speak in different tongues. This continues to be one of the most controversial and misunderstood of all the gifts. When the original outpouring of the Holy Spirit came on Pentecost, all those in the Upper Room began speaking in tongues: *"And they were all filled with the Holy Ghost, and began to speak with other tongues, as the Spirit gave them utterance"* (*Acts 2:4*). The literal translation in Greek is "glossa" and means tongues/languages. This same word "glossa" (language) is used again in *Acts 2:11*. This means it is a known language, not an unknown tongue, but the individual has been supernaturally endowed with the power to speak a language he/she has not studied and does not naturally know.

The Unknown Tongue

I Corinthians 14:2 declares, "*For he that speaketh in an unknown tongue speaketh not unto men, but unto God: for no man understandeth him; howbeit in the spirit he speaketh mysteries.*" Unlike the Gift of Diverse Tongues where individuals are supernaturally endowed to speak in languages they have not studied and do not know, this gift is the ability to speak in what some call "the heavenly language." Here, the believer is speaking directly to God. Among some denominations, this gift is the evidence that an individual has experienced the full measure of the in-filling of the Holy Spirit. *Acts 19:6* declares: "*And when Paul had laid his hands upon them, the Holy Ghost came on them; and they spake with tongues, and prophesied.*"

The Gift of Interpretation of Tongues (Category: Speaking Gift)

The next gift the Apostle Paul mentions is the gift of interpretation of tongues. Using this gift, the believer clearly and accurately reveals the meaning of another tongue or language to other believers.

The Apostle Paul wants the church to understand that all the gifts come from God, and all, working in harmony, are essential to bringing the church to spiritual maturity. Therefore, each gift should be equally respected (*I Corinthians 12:12-23 through I Corinthians 13*).

OTHER SPIRITUAL GIFTS

I n addition to the Gifts of the Spirit covered earlier, the Apostle Paul makes us aware of other giftings, all of which are also bestowed by the Holy Spirit and require Holy Spirit anointing for effective operation. *Romans 12:6-8* speaks of the gifts of serving, teaching, encouraging, giving, and showing mercy. *"Having then gifts differing according to the grace that is given to us, whether prophecy, let us prophesy according to the proportion of faith; Or ministry, let us wait on our ministering: or he that teacheth, on teaching; Or he that exhorteth, on exhortation: he that giveth, let him do it with simplicity; he that ruleth, with diligence; he that sheweth mercy, with cheerfulness."*

Note that in the above text, the Apostle Paul urges the possessor of the gift to not only exercise the gift, but to do so with the proper attitude toward the gift. He makes it clear that the individual must necessarily invest some time in preparation to exercise these gifts ("wait on our ministering", wait on our teaching", wait on our exhortation"). It is interesting he does not say to wait on giving, but encourages the giver to give, doing so with simplicity. The one in charge is to lead with all seriousness. The individual exercising the gift of mercy should do so cheerfully, and not as if it is a challenge to do so. The Apostle Paul further mentions the gifts of helps and governments in *I Corinthians 12:28*.

Some individuals are endowed with the power to do things that are not ordinarily considered gifts. The Apostle Paul would have us know that:

> ➤ These are indeed spiritual giftings
> ➤ They are also bestowed by the Holy Spirit
> ➤ They also require Holy Spirit anointing for operation

It is vital that you seek the face of God so that He reveals your spiritual giftings to you. The gifts were given to you so that you will excel in the ministry God has assigned to you, and to ensure the maximum benefit is received by those to whom you minister.

THE FIVE-FOLD MINISTRY GIFTS (MINISTRY OFFICES)

*E*phesians 4:11 reveals yet more gifts. The Apostle Paul indicates there are apostles, prophets, evangelists, pastors, and teachers. These gifts, or ministry offices, are called the "Ascension Gifts", because Christ gave these offices to the church prior to His ascension. Illustrators have utilized several things to represent these offices and the relationship between them. Very often, a simple picture of the human hand is utilized. Let's take a closer look.

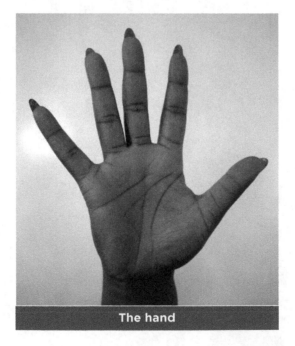

The hand

The Thumb: The Apostle

The thumb has a place of prominence on the hand, both in terms of placement and power. It enjoys the greatest range of motion among all the fingers, and it can easily reach all the rest. Working in harmony, all five make it possible for you to pick up, hold and manipulate objects.

The Apostle is the administrative and foundational layer of the church. As such, this individual's office and function is appropriately represented on the hand by the thumb. Since The Apostle can touch all five of the ministry offices, this individual has the ability to operate in each of the offices. The Apostle is a pioneer, with the power and God-given authority to govern and to bring order to the House of God. Ministries are developed, organized and leaders are installed to continue the work. The Apostle also gives direction for not only the local church ministry, but this individual may lead within the universal church, as well, according to the will and plan of God.

Exercise: Use your thumb to reach each of the other fingers on your hand. Do you notice anything? When the thumb reaches for another finger, that finger will extend itself toward the thumb, even if the movement is slight. Think about the implications this fact has in the spirit realm for the apostle and that relationship to the other ministry offices.

The Index Finger: The Prophet

The index finger or 'pointing finger' as it is often referred to, is called by that term because the majority of individuals use it to point to objects, to give directions, or to make a strong point when speaking. The thumb and index finger have a unique relationship. Together, with the subtle aid of the third finger, they make it possible to do certain actions, such as holding a pen or pencil.

The Prophet, represented by the index finger on the hand, may give a prophetic utterance to individuals, but the message of the true prophet is customarily to the church in general. The message is delivered with authority and often consists of instructions or encouragement for the Body of Christ, or a rebuke. Whatever the nature of the prophetic word, the word of **The Prophet** always has as its end, the goal of moving the church forward and upward.

The Third (middle) Finger: The Evangelist

The third (middle) finger on the hand is the longest. **The Evangelist** is represented by this finger. **The Evangelist** is the one who most often ventures out beyond the church building to reach souls for Christ. In the days of the early church, **The Evangelist** would predominantly travel to foreign lands preaching the Gospel. Noting the increasing need for the Gospel in their own societies, many of today's **Evangelists** focus on spreading the good news of the Gospel at home, rather than traveling to foreign lands. You may find them conducting street revivals, prison services, etc. Some may even be found working in hospitals as chaplains. This individual is gifted to encourage, stir up, and challenge the congregation to embrace the mission and vision of the local church. Given **The Evangelist's** ability to literally change the atmosphere in a service, he/she may be effective on the Praise Team, or in presenting the Invitation to Discipleship following the preaching of The Word.

The Fourth (Ring) Finger: The Pastor

The fourth (ring) finger is thought to be one of the weaker fingers on the hand. On the contrary, it possesses great strength because it lends support to all the other fingers (members) of the hand. **The Pastor**, represented by the fourth finger on the hand, has a heart (deep-rooted, unconditional love) for the people of God. These individuals place such priority on the church that they often appear to have no life of their own. It is no coincidence that **The Pastor** is represented by the finger wearing the ring ... the symbol of a union, an unending relationship. As the shepherd, **The Pastor** is concerned with leading and guarding the flock that God has placed in his/her care.

The Little Finger (Pinkie): The Teacher

Woman holding Bible, teaching stance

The pinkie may be the smallest finger on the hand, but it is by no means insignificant. Extending from the base of your wrist by a muscle called the *hypothenar eminence*, it has substantial dexterity. It is aided by the other fingers in the performance of tasks.

Represented by the little finger on the hand, **The Teacher** is an individual who is driven by the pursuit of truth and understanding the mysteries of God. Further, the teacher is focused on rightly dividing the Word of Truth and relating It to God's people, so they understand it, apply it, and grow from it. In this function, **The Teacher** serves as the grounding force in the ministry, supported by the other ministry offices.

RECOGNIZING THE SPIRITUALLY MATURE CHRISTIAN

It is generally accepted that no one will reach perfection in this life. It is possible, however, and fully expected, that all who have accepted Christ as Lord and Savior will consistently grow in grace. God expects us to put off more of the old man and put on more of the nature of Christ daily. We will examine a few of the many traits the Bible uses to describe the maturing Christian. Preparing for ordination, you will be expected to exhibit the following characteristics, as each of them is evident in the maturing Christian:

Characteristic	Description
The Fruit of the Spirit is Evident	Recognizing the spiritually mature person is not difficult. The Bible declares: *"Ye shall know them by their fruits. Do men gather grapes of thorns, or figs of thistles?"* (*Matthew 7:16*)
Has Discernment	The spiritually mature Christian is capable of discerning right from wrong, and they choose to do what is right, even when it is not the most popular position to take.
Is Grounded	The spiritually mature individual is not easily confused or deterred from the faith by false

Characteristic	Description
	teaching. *"Till we all come in the unity of the faith and of the knowledge of the Son of God, unto a perfect man, unto the measure of the stature of the fulness of Christ: That we henceforth be no more children, tossed to and fro, and carried about with every wind of doctrine, by the sleight of men, and cunning craftiness, whereby they lie in wait to deceive;"* (Ephesians 4:13-14). He/She is so firmly planted in the truth of God's Word that false teaching is quickly recognized, and he/she takes a stand against it, irrespective of the direction from which it comes.
Exercises Self-control	The Bible teaches us that the tongue is hard to control. When an individual can control his/her tongue, that person is moving toward maturity in Christ. *"For in many things we offend all. If any man offend not in word, the same is a perfect man, and able to bridle the whole body"* (James 3:2).
Demonstrates Agape Love	The actions and words of the mature Christian will emanate from a heart of love for his/her fellow Christians. He/She will guard against ever deliberately causing offense, but always strive to build up. We are exhorted in 1 John 4:9-11: *"In this was manifested the love of God toward us, because that God sent his only begotten Son into the world, that we might live through him. Herein is love, not that we loved God, but that he loved us, and sent his Son to be the propitiation for our sins. Beloved, if God so loved us we ought also to love one another."*
Lives Life on Purpose	The mature Christian maintains focus because he/she lives life with a view toward eternity and the role he/she plays in preparing others for that eternity. The reality of eternity is the driving force in his/her life.

Characteristic	Description
	"Brethren, I count not myself to have apprehended: but this one thing I do, forgetting those things which are behind, and reaching forth unto those things which are before, I press toward the mark for the prize of the high calling of God in Christ Jesus. Let us therefore as many as be perfect, be thus minded: and if in anything ye be otherwise minded, God shall reveal even this unto you" (Philippians 3:13-15).
Has the Heart of a Servant	Mature Christians will seek to better serve the church rather than their own interests. They are proactive in their efforts to improve the lives of others. *"I have shewed you all things, how that so labouring ye ought to support the weak, and to remember the words of the Lord Jesus, how he said, It is more blessed to give than to receive"* (Acts 20:35).
Is Consistent	The valley experiences in life do not cause the mature Christian to retreat from God or become discouraged. This individual encourages him/ herself with the words from *Psalm 34:19*: *"Many are the afflictions of the righteous: but the LORD delivereth him out of them all."*
Walks by Faith and Not by Sight	In agreement with *II Corinthians 5:7*, mature Christians trust God implicitly. They know that God is their source, not their place of employment or family and friends. It is GOD. Despite what it looks like, despite what it feels like, they no longer look to man first; they go directly and immediately to God.
Demonstrates an Above Average Ability to Relate to Others	Mature Christians "relate" well to others who are yet in the growing process. Understanding that you will never be perfectly mature in Christ until you have been made like Him following the rapture of the church, you must have the ability to empathize with those you will be leading. Congregants must

Characteristic	Description
	be able o feel that you identify with their current position, and not feel you are judging them, whether you speak judgmental words or not. You must embrace your life experiences (even the most unpleasant) to give depth to your work in the ministry.
Is Genuine	It has been said that some of the most intelligent people can be found in the audience. If you are not sincere and genuine in your approach to and delivery of ministry, your audience will be able to recognize it, despite your best efforts to conceal it. If you are perceived as insincere, you will not reap the maximum benefits of your work. Being genuine and sincere is of the utmost importance.
Is Skilled at Resolving Conflicts	There are several approaches to dealing with conflict, and each minister does so according to his/her personality, training, attitude toward people and his/her own self-concept. Some prefer to avoid conflict altogether. They would rather avoid the temporary discomfort of boldly confronting the conflict situation. Avoidance will only result in a compromise of personal standards, the perpetuation of the devil's divisive tactics, and the hindrance of God's plan for your ministry. Still others believe they can resolve conflict by taking the back seat, putting their own feelings and interests aside for the sake of peace. They believe this causes them to earn the title of "peace makers" and thereby be known as the children of God. In reality, they are allowing the enemy free reign … not at all what God intended.
Where are YOU On the Spiritual Maturity Spectrum?	Another approach to resolving conflicts is found in the individual who seeks his/her own needs above those of the other person(s) in the conflict situation. It is important that those engaged in

Characteristic	Description
	conflict resolution seek the solution that will benefit all parties involved (a "win-win" solution).
	If a "win-win" solution is to be achieved, each side must be willing to listen to the other and make some concessions. Seek the will of God in all circumstances. God is a God of peace. Therefore, seek peace, for the Word of God declares, *"Follow peace with all men, and holiness, without which no man shall see the Lord."* (Hebrews 12:14).
	Which is characteristic of you … most of the time? How you manage conflict on a personal level will affect how you lead others in conflict resolution on a personal level and within the ministry.

Remember that whatever your life experiences have been up to this point, they all had a purpose. The good, the bad and the ugly events, encounters, successes, and failures, even the times you would characterize as a total derailment by the enemy were all necessary. They were either sent or allowed by a sovereign God to mold, shape, prepare, and equip you to be the most effective servant possible. They were used by God to bring you to the point you are today, and God is not yet finished with those events in your life. He will re-use them in conjunction with your present and future circumstances to help you arrive at your place of destiny.

Romans 8:28 reminds us, *"And we know that all things work together for good to them that love God, to them who are the called according to his purpose."* God's blueprint for your life is specific and detailed. Being omniscient, He knew before you were born what would be necessary for you to become His ideal servant. He knew everyone you would encounter and everything those individuals would need you to be if you are to influence their destinies. So do not judge your mistakes and blunders too harshly. God is using your mistakes, missteps, and wrong turns for your benefit and the eternal benefit of others.

It does not matter that you do not see the whole picture at this point in your life and ministry. It will all be revealed in God's perfect timing. Many challenges will come your way along your journey. When you find yourself wondering why, take a moment and remind yourself of the truth in *II Timothy 3:12*: *"Yea, and all that will live godly in Christ Jesus shall suffer persecution."*

When you find yourself tempted to complain, remind yourself that the Holy Spirit is your personal paraclete, walking alongside you in all you go through. When you walk through the fire, He is beside you. When you attempt to navigate through flood waters, He is with you. When you experience wilderness experiences, He sustains you. When you are on the mountain top, He is there, as well, helping you rejoice in your season of blessing. Your challenge is to simply trust God from a position of child-like faith. Trust Him to know what it takes to make certain you arrive at the unique destiny He has reserved for you in this life and in the life to come. As you do so, you bring glory to His name and attract His favor upon your life.

PERSONAL CHARACTERISTICS ESSENTIAL FOR EFFECTIVE MINISTRY

All too often people make the mistake of thinking that all we need is the gifting and anointing of the Holy Spirit to experience success in ministry. What we must recognize, however, is that our **personal "selves"** will have a **great influence** on how we operate within the gifting and anointing. That is one of the reasons we have insisted on introspection all along your path to ordination. Examine your motives, skill sets and personal traits often.

Let's take a brief look at twelve major characteristics deemed essential if any minister is to experience optimum yields in ministry.

EMOTIONAL MATURITY

Emotional maturity occurs when one understands and is in control of his/her emotions.

Individuals who are emotionally mature display balance in their emotions. They do not engage in irrational or erratic behaviors, but accept that they are human and will experience love, anger, hurt, etc. They understand that there will be "highs and lows" in life, and that situations will arise to challenge them. The emotionally mature will not "fall apart," run away, throw temper tantrums, or allow people or circumstances to "push their buttons". Their response to these situations, will be to remain steadfast and confident in who they are and to Whom they belong. The emotionally mature individuals have no need to constantly defend themselves or seek the vindication of others when they have been challenged. They are not defined by man, but by their Creator.

SPIRITUAL MATURITY

Spiritual maturity refers to an individual's steadfastness in God and consistent commitment to his/her divine assignment. This individual is not easily distracted nor discouraged (two of the enemy's most effective weapons). The leader demonstrates integrity of character, is kind, loving and approachable. This person is also able to discern the difference between right and wrong, the intents of others, and the best direction for the people of God. This individual can give God praise despite circumstances that come to challenge his/her faith. Again, we refer you to *Ephesians 4:14*: *"That we henceforth be no more children, tossed to and fro, and carried about with every wind of doctrine, by the sleight of men, and cunning craftiness, whereby they lie in wait to deceive;"* This individual also recognizes the need to be a life-long learner.

BALANCE

The effective contemporary leader will see the value of balance in his/her life and the lives of others. He/She recognizes that God has priorities, and as a partner with Christ in ministry, there must be prioritization but balance, as well. The absence of balance leaves room for family neglect, for example, or the lack of rest and rejuvenation for the physical man. Taking care of the body (the temple of God) will ensure that the physical can meet the challenges required of it. It will also serve to demonstrate to others the fact that the individual values him/herself. Showing you place value on your own physical man will alleviate the tendency of others to take advantage of you and your giftings.

TRANSPARENCY

The effective contemporary leader is one marked by transparency. He/She can be read as an open book. In other words, he/she is genuine, and to coin a secular phrase, "what you see is what you get." There is no attempt to be something he/she is not, nor masks or facades behind which to hide. The transparent leader willingly admits to having led a life that has not been perfect, but is reaching for God's state of perfection, has accepted the total forgiveness of God, and has forgiven his/her own past. That means the individual has accepted the past, has "moved past the past" and is not bound by the past, but merely uses it to show what the saving grace of a loving God can do.

EMPATHY

Empathy is the ability to relate to others; to understand their feelings; to be able to understand what they are experiencing. Popular opinion is that one cannot relate to another's problem unless he/she has endured the exact same issues. It is critical that we trust that the Holy Spirit has all knowledge and can impart knowledge and understanding beyond our life experiences when needed. Leaders in contemporary society **MUST** be able to relate to the various levels of fear, anxiety, frustration, and loss that contemporary society experiences today. If those being ministered to feel the absence of empathy, they may be hesitant to share their vulnerability with the leader. The ability to relate assists the leader in recognizing the direction that must be taken for the greater good of the person(s) being ministered to. Without this "relatability" the leader will miss the opportunity to provide "real ministry" … which is deliverance of the "**whole man**." Jesus came to bring us abundant life. That cannot happen until deliverance of the whole man is a reality.

EMBRACES CHANGE

If leaders are to be effective in contemporary society, they must embrace change. There is nothing wrong in honoring and preserving traditional values. Yet, leaders must be willing and able to adapt their leadership style and operational policies to provide a welcoming atmosphere. This does **NOT** mean, however, that biblical standards are compromised.

SPIRITUAL CREATIVITY

The effective leader will be an atmosphere changer. This involves two major abilities. The first is the ability to "usher in the Spirit". This is particularly valuable during worship services where it seems the enemy is hindering the service from going forth as God desires. The creative leader will recognize the hindrance and battle in the spirit realm to release the move of God's Spirit in the atmosphere.

Secondly, the effective leader will find ways to make the scriptures and worship experience "come alive" (manifest relevancy) to all worshippers. This is particularly valuable when ministering to the younger generation.

MULTI-DIMENSIONAL

In many ministries today, we are seeing increasing diversity in terms of attendance. Changes in laws have had a dramatic effect on how ministry is delivered, as well. This means that the effective leaders must be increasingly flexible in their thinking and styles. This will enable them to guide individuals from diverse ethnic and experiential backgrounds to conversion and maturity in Christ. Different cultures require different techniques. This, in turn, requires a knowledge of those ethnicities, a complete openness to the Spirit of God, and a non-judgmental attitude.

MOTIVATIONAL AND INSPIRATIONAL

The effective leader, under the influence of the Spirit of God, serves as the outer motivating force for individuals to seek the change that is needed in their lives. The leader can light the person's inner spark of inspiration. The result is that the person follows through on their journey to reaching their God-given destiny. This is done as the leader minsters the Word, is an example in word and deed, and daily "walks out" the motivation and inspiration he/she is trying to pass on to others. Given time and involvement of the Spirit of God, motivation and inspiration are contagious!

BUILDER

The effective leader in contemporary society must be a builder in two major areas. First, he/she must be a builder of people. The successful ministry will be the one focusing on the health of ministry members, not the leader. The leader must be fully aware of his/her ability to either build up or tear down an individual through his/her words, actions, and attitudes. *Proverbs 18:21* reminds us, *"Death and life are in the power of the tongue: and they that love it shall eat the fruit thereof."* It must be remembered that once words are spoken, they can bring harm or healing and health. Once hurtful words are spoken, they can never be retracted, even though apologies may be offered afterward.

Secondly, the leader must be a builder of ministry itself. He/She must have the ability to take a group of individuals from where they are and lead them to a higher plane through revelation knowledge that can only come from the Spirit Himself.

VISIONARY

The effective leader will **have a vision** from God regarding the direction and focus of the ministry. The visionary is rather like a dreamer, like the young, 17-year-old Joseph in *Genesis 37*, who had dreams of his brothers bowing down to him. Like many of us with dreams and visions, he was eager to share them with others. What the young Joseph did not realize, however, was that his brothers were not as elated as he was to hear about the substance of his dreams. Many of us today have the "Joseph syndrome" and feel we simply **MUST** share any and everything God reveals to us... often to our detriment. This is because we open ourselves up for an unexpected attack from the enemy. Pray before you share the totality of your vision.

While the scripture states that where there is no vision the people perish (*Proverbs 29:18*), some visions are to be shared in the moment, others are to be shared later, but all must be delivered following explicit instructions from the Lord. As a leader you must have a vision...one which you can lay out in a clear, concise manner that will give the people direction and a goal to work toward for the advancement of the Kingdom on earth. Human nature requires that people have a noble goal to keep them focused, interested, and engaged, naturally and spiritually.

The second point that must be made regarding the visionary is that he/she must **have vision**. That means he/she must have spiritual insight, be able to see the enemy's coming attacks, be able to discern the difference between an attack of the enemy and life challenges and possess the spiritual eye to see beyond the moment to the manifestation of the vision. This vision produces the joy of the Lord, which in turn results in sustaining strength, stamina, and patience.

TEAM MEMBER

The contemporary leader must be a member of the team, not an authoritarian who merely gives "marching" orders and stands back waiting for the "troops" to do all the work. The leader must be leader enough to lead by example, but also humble enough to join in and get his/her hands dirty with the work of the ministry whenever necessary.

PART III

—

JOB DESCRIPTIONS

RESPONSIBILITIES OF ORDAINED MINISTERS

Female minister pointing upward while preaching

The duties of the ordained minister will be multi-faceted, requiring you to wear many hats. Among the major ones are pastor, counselor, prayer warrior, and community outreach worker. Let's take a closer look at these four hats.

Pastor: The pastor's position consists of many combined roles, including but not limited to preacher/teacher, counselor, prayer warrior, community outreach worker, trainer, and confidant.

Preaching the Word of God with power and anointing; rightly dividing the Word of Truth …

The Pastor:

➤ Delivers sermons to the congregation on a weekly basis that edify members of the congregation individually and collectively
➤ Serves as the main source of scriptural and doctrinal teaching and interpretation

> ➤ Serves as the spiritual covering for the flock
> ➤ Is the main source of spiritual growth and development of the congregation
> ➤ Oversees/officiates celebrations such as baby christenings, baptisms, weddings, funerals, etc. for the congregation and the community
> ➤ Interprets and guides the congregation through the fulfillment of the vision and mission of the ministry
> ➤ Serves as an ex-officio member of all ministries within the congregation and as the moderator for all church governing board and congregational meetings.

You are expected to have teaching skills, enabling you to make scriptures clear to the congregation. When scripture is unclear, congregants cannot be expected to make the proper application of scripture to their lives. When proper application is not achieved, spiritual growth is retarded.

If you are not the pastor, you can help lighten the pastor's burden in a variety of ways. Ordained ministers are expected to share the burden the pastor carries for the ministry. As a member of the pastor's team of leaders, your responsibility is to assist the pastor in every way possible, and to be an example in every area of your life. The ministerial team functions as the pastor's supporters, and in a broad sense, is his/her personal team of armor bearers. To be effective, you must make yourself available to the pastor and other members of the ministerial team when needed.

Other key points to remember:

> ➤ God's business must be your priority
> ➤ Like Christ, you must love your brothers and sisters unconditionally
> ➤ Your faithfulness to the church and loyalty to your pastor are crucial to the success of the ministry, and should never be questioned
> ➤ Good communication and bonding among leadership must be maintained

> ➤ Laziness or slothfulness cannot be tolerated if the ministry is to flourish
> ➤ Organization in your personal life is a must
> ➤ Your consistency is vital to the flourishing of the ministry and your own growth and development.

Counselor:

Christian counselor consulting the Bible while counseling

Ministers are often counselors to the hurting and mourning members of the church, as well as individuals outside of the church. They offer comfort in times of crisis, support in employment searches, and guidance in resolving a myriad of personal conflicts people encounter, as individuals and as families. Often, these services are informal in nature and resemble "lending an ear."

At other times, these services are more formalized and extensive. Whatever the nature of the interaction, this counseling service demands the same level of confidentiality that licensed, credentialed psychologists or clinical therapists must extend to their patients in the secular world.

Congregants or non-members who come seeking counseling services must be made to feel it is safe for them to become vulnerable with you.

If you are unable to establish a trust relationship with the individual you are counseling, you will not be able to meet the deeper needs of the individual. Trust in you as a helper must be established first. The counselees must sense that you have unconditional regard for them, have not established any advanced judgments of them, cannot be shocked by what they may share with you, and that all they share will be held in the strictest confidence.

Prayer Warrior:

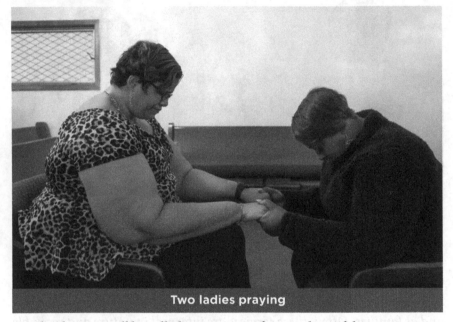

Two ladies praying

As a leader, you will be called upon to pray for members of the congregation and non-members alike. Be always ready.

Once ordained, you may be referred to by any of the following titles, depending upon your religious denomination or association: Reverend, Elder, Pastor, Minister, Brother, or Sister. Do not allow yourself to be concerned about not being called by your ordained title. If you are, re-evaluate your motives.

Congregants will look to you more readily for prayer and may seek you out to relieve the Senior Pastor of some of the burden once your ordination takes place. You will be asked to pray for members of the church, for their friends and their family members. Congregants can call you to pray even when you are not at the church. You must be ready to offer prayer, with the assurance that you have lived a life that pleases God. You can then be confident your prayer will be heard and answered.

Prayer Line

When people are sick, they will call upon you for prayer based on *James 5:14-16*. Rest assured, the calls will not come when it is convenient for you or your family. In fact, they will come at the **MOST INOPPORTUNE** times … and you will have to go … rain, sleet, or blinding snow.

Community Outreach:

Each church has an "extended church" which is the neighborhood where the church building is located. Ordained ministers are to find ways to assist the church in becoming involved in the community and ways to involve the community in the church. This may not come without some challenges; however, it must be viewed as an extension of the hand of God. Feeding, clothing and otherwise showing the love of Christ to the homeless, mis-guided youth and troubled adults, are further responses to the clarion call issued by Christ in the great commission.

The Bible teaches us we will be judged for how we responded to the needs of the less fortunate while on earth. Refer to *Matthew 25:41-46*, where Jesus gives us a glimpse of the judgment. In this parable, Jesus sends those away who had not served the least ones by feeding the hungry, giving water to the thirsty, clothing the naked, sheltering he stranger, visiting the sick or incarcerated. When the "church goers" asked when they failed to serve the Lord in this manner, his response was that what they failed to do for the least ones was not done for Him. The result was they were cast from the presence of God into outer darkness.

As a leader, you must be seen as a living example of how we are to serve God's people. Are you willing to go into the trenches and seek the lost? The photo below presents an idea of how we may show the love of God in our community.

Two ladies looking at clothing

You will have numerous opportunities to demonstrate the love and character of Christ in your new position. Will you be an individual who will be hesitant to reach out to those whom society has turned its back on? Or will you be the individual who is eager to bring health, healing, and comfort to those who have lost their way and are on the brink of hopelessness? Will your attitude reflect the mind of Christ as He stated: *"Even as the Son of man came not to be ministered unto, but to minister, and to give his life a ransom for many"* (*Matthew 20:28*).

RESPONSIBILITIES OF ORDAINED DEACONS

Deacons and Pastors are the only two church offices presented in the Bible. Deacons play a vital role in the church, since they work in numerous capacities to keep the church operating. Although some denominations consider them ministers, they typically do not deliver sermons, except on special occasions, or when no minister is available. The word deacon means servant, and the individual with a deacon's heart is one of the hardest working people in the ministry of the local church. At the direction of the pastor, and based upon their talents, abilities and interests, their duties may include any or all the following:

- ➢ assisting with weddings
- ➢ assisting with funeral services
- ➢ assisting with Holy Communion
- ➢ visiting the sick
- ➢ making bereavement calls
- ➢ visiting the incarcerated
- ➢ mediating conflicts
- ➢ organizing various ministry areas
- ➢ training the Diaconate
- ➢ assisting with member emergencies
- ➢ involvement in outreach
- ➢ assessing ministry needs
- ➢ ensuring that the ministry facilities and grounds are appropriately maintained

Prayer Warrior

The ordained deacon is expected to live a life of prayer and consecration so that he may assist the ministerial staff in whatever capacity needed. In the role of deacon, you will be called upon to pray for members of the church, members of their family or community residents.

Ministry Leadership

The ordained deacon must be capable of stepping up into a leadership position when necessary. In the event no member of the ministerial staff is available or there is no pastor, the ordained deacon is the next in line to assume leadership of the ministry. For optimum effectiveness, deacons must have developed a good working relationship with the congregation and be respected by the community at large. The Apostle Paul spells out the qualifications for deacons in *1 Timothy 3:8 and Titus 1*. It is a good practice to periodically review these qualifications and assess how you are continuing to measure up:

"Likewise must the deacons be grave, not double-tongued, not given to much wine, not greedy of filthy lucre; Holding the mystery of the faith in a pure conscience. And let these also first be proved; then let them use the office of a deacon, being found blameless. Even so must their wives be grave, not slanderers, sober, faithful in all things. Let the deacons be the husbands of one wife, ruling their children and their own houses well."

Remember that whether you are at your home church or visiting at another, you are never separate from your position as a deacon. You have stepped into the position. You have put it on as if it were an article of clothing. Therefore, you must be among the first to follow order … your position demands it because you REPRESENT ORDER. You should look like the servant that you are, and the atmosphere around you should reflect your position. How you conduct yourself should command respect in all places and circumstances. Despite where you are, no one should ever have to speculate on your role in ministry, your dedication to your local church, or your commitment to the cause of Christ. You are a deacon.

PART IV

—

FOUNDATIONAL TRUTHS
(THE ARTICLES OF FAITH: WHAT WE BELIEVE)

THE ARTICLES OF FAITH
(WHAT WE BELIEVE)

In addition to their church constitution and detailed set of by-laws, most churches have adopted a set of fundamental beliefs which guide them in structuring the teachings and general operation of the ministry. These beliefs are therefore fundamental and may be referred to when determining policies and ministry direction. Familiarize yourself with this document. It is often included in the material candidates for ordination are expected to know during the oral examination by the Council.

These beliefs may be given a variety of titles including, but not limited to: Articles of Religion, Articles of Faith, Statement of Faith, or simply, "What We Believe." What follows is a sample "Articles of Religion".

"Articles of Religion"

ARTICLE 1   **THE DIVINE INSPIRATION OF THE SCRIPTURES**

The Holy Bible, (both the Old and New Testaments), is the divinely inspired Word of God, infallible, entirely trustworthy, and serves as the rule of faith and source of ethical conduct. Believers should commit to a lifetime of studying the Word of God for the perfecting of their spiritual growth.

Scripture References
II Timothy 3:15-17
II Timothy 2:15
John 8:32
Joshua 1:8

ARTICLE 2   THE ONE TRUE GOD

There is one true God with an everlasting existence who reserves the right of uncontestable sovereignty. Through His omnipotent and omnipresent characteristics, God reveals Himself to man as God, the Father; as Jesus Christ, the Son of God (the Word of God in flesh); and the Holy Spirit.

Scripture References
Deuteronomy 6:4
Mark 12:29
I John 5:7
John 1:1-14
Isaiah 43:10-11

ARTICLE 3   THE DEITY OF THE LORD JESUS CHRIST

The Lord Jesus Christ is the eternal Son of God. The Scriptures declare:
- His virgin birth
- His sinless life
- His miracles
- His atoning work on the cross
- His bodily resurrection from the dead and exaltation to the right hand of God

Scripture References
Matthew 1:23
Luke 1:31-35
Hebrews 7:26

I Peter 2:22
Acts 2:22; 10:38
I Corinthians 15:3
II Corinthians 5:21
Matthew 28:6
Luke 2
Acts 1:9, 11; 2:33
Philippians 2:9-11

ARTICLE 4   THE FALL AND SALVATION OF MAN

Man was created good and upright; for God said, *"Let us make man in our image, after our likeness."* However, by voluntary transgression, man fell, and thereby incurred not only physical death, but also spiritual death, which is separation from God. There is salvation for every lost and sinful man. Salvation is acquired through confession and belief in the life, death, and resurrection of Jesus Christ as the true Messiah.

Scripture References
Genesis 1:26-27; 2:17; 3:6
Romans 5:12-19
John 3:16
Romans 10:7-10

ARTICLE 5   THE BAPTISM IN THE HOLY SPIRIT

All believers are entitled to and should earnestly seek the promise of the Father, the baptism in the Holy Spirit, according to the command of our Lord Jesus Christ. With it comes the enduement of power for life and service, the bestowing of the gifts of the Spirit and their use in the work of the ministry This experience is distinct from and subsequent to the experience of the new birth.

With the baptism in the Holy Spirit come such experiences as an overflowing fullness of the Spirit, a deepened reverence for God, an intensified consecration to God and dedication to His work, and a more active love for Christ, for His Word, and for the lost. The baptism of believers in the Holy Spirit may also be witnessed by the physical sign of speaking with other tongues as the Spirit of God gives them utterance. The speaking in tongues in this instance is the same, in essence, as the gift of tongues, but different in purpose and use.

The transformed life and the "Fruit of the Spirit" is the greatest evidence of the baptism inf the Holy Spirit.

A lifestyle of sanctification is an act of separation from that which is evil, and of dedication unto God. Scriptures teach a life of "holiness without which no man shall see the Lord". By the power of the Holy Spirit, we can obey the command: "Be ye holy, for I am holy". Sanctification is realized in the believer by recognizing his identification with Christ in His death and resurrection. Sanctification can be realized by daily renewing the mind and by offering the mind and body continually to the dominion of the Holy Spirit.

Man must sanctify himself from: violence, criminal activity, lies, vulgarity, drunkenness, adultery, fornication, sexual perversion/lasciviousness, and abuse of drugs.

Scripture References
Acts 10:44-46
Acts 19:6
Galatians 5:16-26

I Corinthians 6:19
Hebrews 12:14
I Peter 1:15-16
Ephesians 4:24
Luke 24:49
Acts 8:12-17
John 7:37-39
Hebrews 12:28
Acts 2:42
Mark 16:20
Acts 2:4
I Corinthians 12:4-10; 28
Romans 12:1-2
Hebrews 12:14
I Peter 1:15-16
Romans 6:1-11
Galatians 2:20

ARTICLE 6   DIVINE HEALING

Divine healing is an integral part of the Gospel. Deliverance from sickness is provided for in the atonement, and it is the privilege of all believers.

Scripture References
Isaiah 53:4-5
Matthew 8:16-17
James 5:14-16

ARTICLE 7   DIVINE DELIVERANCE

Deliverance is a privilege from God and empowered by the Holy Spirit, through fasting and prayer. Divine Deliverance will set possessed and oppressed individuals free from demonic spirits and/or the bondage of social ills.

Scripture References
John 8:36
Matthew 17:14-21
Mark 5:1-13

ARTICLE 8 THE RETURN OF CHRIST

The return of Christ includes the rapturing of the saints, which is our blessed hope of eternal life, world without end.

Scripture References
I Thessalonians 4:13-18
I Corinthians 15:51-58
Revelation 21:1-5

ARTICLE 9 THE FINAL JUDGMENT

There will be a final judgment in which the wicked will be judged according to their works. Whosoever is not found written in the Book of Life, together with the devil and his angels, the beast and the false prophet, will be consigned to everlasting punishment.

Scripture References
Matthew 25:46
Mark 9:43-50
Revelation 19:20
Revelation 20:11-15; 21:8
Psalm 9:17

ARTICLE 10 PRAYER

A commitment to Prayer is the believer's divine and continuous connection to the Almighty God.

Scripture References
James 5:16
II Thessalonians 5:17

ARTICLE 11 PRAISE AND WORSHIP

A commitment to Praise and Worship is a privilege of the believer to please the Almighty God.

Scripture References
Psalm 100:4; Psalm 34:4 Psalm 150
II Chronicles 5:11-14
John 4:23

ARTICLE 12 CHURCH MEMBERSHIP

Church membership provides believers with fellowship, spiritual growth, evangelism, and outreach.

Scripture References
Luke 14:23
Hebrews 10:23-25
Psalm 27:4
Psalm 133:1

ARTICLE 13 GIVING AND SOWING

A commitment to financial support of the church in tithes and offerings is important to the success of the church and the fruitfulness of the believer.

Scripture References
Genesis 8:22
Malachi 3:8-19
Luke 6:38
Colossians 3:22-25
II Corinthians 9:7

ARTICLE 14   ORDINANCES OF THE CHURCH

<u>Baptism in Water</u>: Water Baptism is a public declaration of a new believer; symbolically being buried and resurrected into a new life in the Lord Jesus Christ. All who repent of their sins, confess Jesus as Lord, and believe in the resurrection of Christ qualify to be baptized in the authority of the Lord Jesus Christ.

<u>Holy Communion</u>: Participation in The Lord's Supper, is the right and privilege of all believers to express our sharing the divine nature of our Lord Jesus Christ, a memorial of His suffering and death, and a prophecy of His second coming till He comes again! Sharing in Holy Communion we remind ourselves of the price Jesus paid for our salvation.

<u>Foot Washing</u>: Symbolizes Christ-like humility and servanthood.

<u>Scripture References</u>
Colossians 2:12
Acts 10:47-48
Acts 2:35-38
Acts 19:3-5
Romans 6:3-5
Matthew 28:19
I Corinthians 11:23-30
John 6:53-58
John 13:2-7

ARTICLE 15   HOLY MATRIMONY

Holy Matrimony is the covenant made between a man and a woman to live faithfully and lovingly married until death separates them, or until sin interferes with the individuals' ability to successfully remain married to each other.

Scripture References
Genesis 2:21-25
Genesis 3:16
Ephesians 5:22-33
Colossians 3:18-19
Mark 10:1-12
Deuteronomy 24:1-4

ARTICLE 16   LAYING ON OF HANDS

Laying on of Hands by the Elders of the Church should not be a sudden action, but reverently executed as a point of contact to impart the anointing of the Holy Spirit for various purposes within the ministry of the Church.

Scripture References
Genesis 48:13-20 (for blessings
Mark 16:18 and James 5:14 (for healing)
Acts 8:14-19 and Acts 19:6 (to receive the Holy Spirit)
I Timothy 4:14-11
II Timothy 1:6 (for affirmation of gifts)
I Timothy 5:22 (*"Lay hands suddenly on no man"*)

ARTICLE 17   CHILD BLESSING

Blessing of Children is a sacred time to publicly acknowledge children as gifts from God; ask the Lord for help to be adequate and Godly parents; and to commit to raising the child in an appropriate Christian atmosphere.

Scripture References
Matthew 18:1-6
Psalm 127:3-5
Proverbs 22:6

ARTICLE 18   BURIAL OF THE DEAD

Committal of the Dead celebrates the life of the sleeping saint and reminds the living that it is precious for the saint to die in the Lord, and that to be absent from the body is to be present with the Lord. Committal of the Dead is also a time to bring comfort to the living.

Scripture References
II Corinthians 5:8
Revelation 14:13
I Thessalonians 4:13-18

PART V

—

THE LOGISTICS OF
MINISTRY

(ORDER IN THE CHURCH)

ORDER IN THE CHURCH

I f God is to be glorified in our churches, we must demonstrate a respect for the church edifice. It is essential that we remember it is His House, after all. In the natural, you would not visit another human being and disrespect his/her home. You honor and respect the rules set forth by the owners of the house you are visiting. We should certainly treat the Lord's house with even greater respect. This is because the church building is where God meets with the assembly of believers. From the beginning, God has designated a specific place to meet with His people. This location, then, is considered hallowed ground in God's eyes, and should be treated as such by leaders and congregants. It is up to you as a leader to instill the necessity of this reverence into those you are leading.

The following scripture clearly expresses God's desire for order in His house, and will serve as our theme for this section:

"Let all things be done decently and in order."
I Corinthians 14:40

Prior to exploring order in the church, it may be beneficial to define some of the terms that will be presented in the text.

Definition of Terms

CHURCH	The New Testament terminology for "church" is: Ekklesia, which simply means "the called-out ones." In studying the New Testament, we discover that ekklesia is used 109 times to identify groups of God's people.
CHURCH EDIFICE	A specific location where people customarily gather to worship God.
ETIQUETTE	The customary rules of comportment or behavior identified as polite in contemporary society. Church Etiquette, then, consists of the customary guidelines for conducting ourselves in the House of God.
PROTOCOL	The behavior or set of procedures deemed acceptable for events such as official ceremonies.
PLATFORM OR DIAS	The elevated area in the front of the church sanctuary. It is the area where we find the Pulpit and special seats for the ministerial staff. Although it is often mistakenly referred to as the "Pulpit", it is not the Pulpit, but a location FOR the Pulpit.
PULPIT	A part of the Platform, the Pulpit is the podium behind which the minister is to stand and deliver the Word of God. It is often referred to as the "Sacred Desk" for this reason. As such, it is the most significant article of furniture in the entire church building. It is centrally located, for this reason.

The special place occupied by the Pulpit is symbolic of the critical nature of the Word of God being delivered from it. Its elevation over the congregation symbolizes how the Word of God being delivered from it covers the people receiving the Word.

Until recent years, Pulpits were primarily constructed of wood. This act symbolized the strength, power, and enduring nature of God's Word as the church's foundation and the standard for perfecting the people of God. Although constructed of various other materials in contemporary society, the Pulpit retains its original meaning as the focal point of the sanctuary.

The minister was expected to stand behind the Pulpit until he/she had completed his/her delivery of the Word of God. By so doing, the minister is symbolically "hiding" him/herself behind the Word he/she is delivering. It was believed this helped the congregation to remain focused and receive the message. In many of today's churches, the minister delivering the Word will often move about during the delivery. This movement is considered a gesture, and like any other gesture that is over-utilized, it may detract from the effectiveness of delivery.

ORDER IN THE CHURCH

The Practice of Good Pulpit Etiquette and Protocol
~ For Ordained Ministers, Deacons, and the Laity ~

Honoring the Sanctuary

Some basic guidelines for honoring the sanctuary, whether at your home church or visiting another ministry include:

1. **TIMELINESS.** Most people who are employed know the importance of arriving at work on time. Just as your tardiness (without a legitimate excuse) shows a disregard for your company and the position you hold, your disregard for punctuality at worship services indicates your lack of respect for God as your employer, and the position you hold in ministry. You may miss valuable opportunities to be greatly used of God if you are late. If you cannot avoid being late, inform the pastor as soon as humanly possible.

2. **A REVERENT ENTRANCE AND EXIT.** Enter or exit the sanctuary quietly and with reverence (a deep respect). Remember, you are in the presence of God. You are in **HIS** House, and it must be honored and respected. Avoid entering or leaving during the:

    *   Prayer
    *   Scripture reading

- Sermon (or whenever a minister is speaking)
- Altar call
- Benediction

If you are at your local church, you should be well-acquainted with the protocol for entering and exiting the sanctuary. If it is necessary that you leave the sanctuary during the worship service, make every effort to avoid causing a distraction to the service, including the time you leave and the door by which you exit. Of course, everyone should remain in church until the closing benediction or final prayer has been offered. If an emergency arises and you must leave, the Usher may remind you of certain procedures. If that happens, respect the Usher as the gatekeeper in the church and respond respectfully. Remember that the congregants will observe your behavior as a model to follow.

3. **RESPECTING GOD'S HOUSE WITH YOUR SILENCE.** You should come prepared to take an active part in the worship experience. Personal, carnal conversations, use of electronic devices, unnecessary walking or passing notes, is unacceptable and most disrespectful to the Lord's house.

4. **GUARDING YOUR SPEECH.** Whether you are in a formal worship service, Bible Study Class, training component, auxiliary meeting, or just passing through for some reason, you should always be aware of the language you utilize in the Lord's House. There should never be any vulgarity or use of vulgarity substitutes in the sanctuary or any other part of the church building.

5. **CONSUME FOOD AND BEVERAGES IN DESIGNATED AREAS ONLY.** No one is to consume food, beverages or chewing gum or candy in the sanctuary. This should be done only in the multi-purpose room or some other area within the facility that has been designated for that purpose. If you have medical reasons for requiring gum or a hard candy during the service, bring it unwrapped in a container to avoid disturbing the service as you

unwrap it. This is permissible for individuals with medical issues, or a cough requiring use of an occasional cough drop or hard candy.

Most churches will have water available for the congregation's use. Juice, soft drinks, etc., have no place in the sanctuary. It is distracting to others who are trying to enjoy the worship experience, and you run the risk of soiling the pew covering or carpeting. Some ministries allow congregants to freely avail themselves of water, while others prefer to have the Ushers or Nurses distribute water. Follow the policy established by your ministry or the ministry you are visiting.

6. **IF YOU ARE THE GUEST SPEAKER.**

Unless unavoidable, you should never arrive late as a guest speaker. Arriving prior to the beginning of the service allows you to be present and involved in the service. Your involvement helps to orient you to the flow of the Spirit in the service. This will have a positive impact on your effectiveness as you minister.

Not only does your tardiness show a deep lack of respect for the pastor and the church you are visiting, it also reflects negatively on the training you have received through your own ministry. It raises concerns about the standards by which your ministry operates. If you **MUST** be late, it is good policy to inform the pastor of the ministry you are visiting. If you are being sent to a church as a representative of your own church or pastor and must be late:

Contact your pastor and ask that the pastor of the church be notified of your unavoidable late arrival. This not only demonstrates respect for your own leader, concern for the reputation of your church, and regard for the leader of the other congregation, it also allows you to follow protocol. Order in the church also encompasses the lines of communication between church leaders.

For example, Pastors should communicate with Pastors, Diaconate Chairs with Diaconate Chairs, Lay members with Lay members, etc. Let's be more specific.

Example: You are a minister at your church, and you are planning a special worship service or some other event. You would like to invite the Diaconate Board of XYZ Church to attend and serve in the Diaconate capacity. A letter of invitation should be developed from the Diaconate Chair of your church to the Diaconate Chair of XYZ Church. The letter should be signed by your Diaconate Chair and yourself, as the event sponsor. Your pastor's name should be placed at the bottom of the letter (as well as his/her signature if he/she desires to affix his/her signature). Your pastor's name on the letter indicates that he/she is aware and approves of the special event and the invitation. It also denotes a clear respect for the other pastor and the rules of order. The pastor of the invited Diaconate Board should, from a respect level, receive a copy of the letter of invitation.

1. **ENTERING AND EXITING THE SANCTUARY.**

Use whatever doors are designated for entering and leaving. Show the same reverence you would at your home church.

2. **USHERS AND GREETERS.**

Many ministries have "Ushers" or "Greeters" at or near the entrance to give directions regarding seating. As a visitor, you will be seated in the audience. If you are the invited speaker, a special guest, or expecting to sit in the front of the sanctuary or on the Platform, introduce yourself to the Usher, and he/she will lead you to the designated place or seat reserved for you.

In some ministries, the clergy meet in the pastor's study and enter the service together. If this is the protocol at this ministry, following the leading of the Usher or Greeter cannot be over-emphasized.

Honoring the Platform and Pulpit

Platform and Pulpit decorum is a learned behavior that must become second nature to you in your ministry. Some general points to keep in mind include (whether at your local church or one other than your own):

Before you step onto the Platform

> ➤ **Pray**: ask God to anoint you with His power, use you to His glory, and help you to honor this ministry's Platform. Remember, you need the power of the Spirit if God's purpose is to be accomplished through you. Ask God to shine so brightly through you that the people see only Him and not you. If the people see you ... the wrong person is on display.

> ➤ **Consider the composition of your audience**. Having some knowledge of the congregation is essential if your message is to reach them. They must be able to feel a connection to you and the message you are bringing. This can only happen if they feel you are "relating" to them and their daily challenges. Before you step onto the Platform, ask God to give you insight into the audience to whom you will be ministering. Like it or not, you are in the spotlight, and there is a high level of expectation of you. The waiting congregation is anticipating a Word from God to address their personal struggles, and they believe you have been given what they need. It will only come from a divine move of the Holy Spirit, The "Revelator".

On the Platform

> ➤ Your comportment on the Platform and at the Pulpit can have a dramatic influence on the service, as well as how you are received while you are ministering The Word. It is imperative that your behavior is respectful and reverent in every way.

> ➤ Since everyone on the Platform can be seen by the entire audience, your mannerisms should in no way be offensive,

nor should your behaviors distract the congregation from the service. Avoid whispering to another person on the Platform, motioning to someone in the congregation, reacting to an incident or statement with a negative facial expression, or using electronic devices. These actions on the Platform are just as disrespectful and irreverent as they are when members of the congregation engage in them.

➢ Individuals seated on the Platform should participate in and enhance all aspects of the service from praise and worship, giving in the offering, and supporting the speaker during delivery of The Word. Be involved, but if you are delivering The Word, preserve some energy for ministering.

➢ If you have been asked to do something other than delver The Word, do exactly what you were asked to do. Do not add anything extra like singing a song or sharing your testimony when you were asked to pray, for example. Do what you were asked to do, and then take your seat.

➢ Acknowledge, support, and encourage the pastor who is allowing you to speak from his/her Pulpit, or whatever minister is delivering The Word. Show honor to the other officials and dignitaries, according to their rank and position.

➢ Be attentive to the needs of the pastor and/or other ministers on the Platform.

➢ Remember that there is only one "minister of the hour." When The Word has been delivered, it is out of order for you or anyone else to follow the preached Word with a second "mini-sermon." That is disrespectful to everyone, including the Holy Spirit.

Observing the Sacredness of the Platform and Pulpit

➢ Only the pastor or persons authorized by the pastor should ever be seated on the Platform. Children should be taught from a young age that this is a sacred place and must never be used as a play area. Adults should refrain from unnecessarily walking across or gathering in this area to hold conversations.

➤ If you are a guest minister, never enter the Platform until the pastor is seated and invites you to the Platform.

➤ When the service has ended, and there is time for greeting the congregation, step down out of the Pulpit/Platform area for fellowship. Observe the rules of the ministry in this regard. Some allow greeting the congregation in the altar area; others prefer it be done in another location such as the vestibule or multi-purpose room.

Proper Platform Attire

➤ Although many ministries in contemporary society have relaxed their rules on what may be worn to worship services, it is always a good practice to dress appropriately. If you are in tune with the Holy Spirit, He will lead you in what is and is not appropriate dress. You may also ask the pastor in advance what the dress code is for any service at home or away from your home church. Some ministries yet have a more formal approach to what is appropriate for worship services, particularly for the ministerial staff. Keep in mind that what may be acceptable at your home church may not be acceptable at a different ministry.

It is expected that all members dress in a manner that honors God. Whether the occasion requires a more formal or casual dress code, we should wear our best. We should dress as if we are going to meet the most important person in the world. Who is more important or worthy of honor than God? Brightly colored or "flashy" apparel are inappropriate in the Pulpit and will prove to be a distraction to the audience. As a minister, you should always be clothed in a manner befitting the dignity of your position, whether in worship service, in the grocery store or relaxing in the park.

A higher standard of dress is expected of Bishops, Pastors, Evangelists, etc., particularly at special services (i.e., funerals, anniversaries, and conventions). When you are unsure what the standards are, inquire of your leader or the pastor in charge of the event so that you will be in order.

Your Delivery

> Preach from your convictions. Attempting to preach a message that is not a part of your belief system will be poorly received by the audience. When that happens, they will miss the benefits of your long hours of preparation, and along with it, their opportunity to grow.

> Speak clearly and distinctly. Speak into the microphone so you may be heard without shouting or yelling.

> **Don't race**. Pay attention to the rate of speed with which you speak or read your message. Taking the time to practice your message aloud will make you aware of needing to speed up or slow down. This is especially helpful when you have a specific time limit for your message.

> Stay within the timeframe you have been given to speak and do not go over. If you are in high gear and it is time to close, simply take your seat. It is perfectly acceptable to leave on a "high."

> Be aware that the most educated persons in church often sit in the pews and not on the Platform. You will lose them with excessive use of pause fillers like "er, uh, and amen." Endeavor to pronounce words correctly. Use correct English and grammar to avoid offending your audience with your words.

> Avoid the use of slang in any form.

> Watch your gestures. We all make gestures when we talk, realize it or not. Gestures can be beneficial in emphasizing what we

are trying to say when preaching, as well. On the other hand, excessive use of gestures is distracting. Some preachers sway constantly, put their hands in their pockets, jingle their change, or make awkward sounds. Excessive gestures or actions that come across as nervous habits will result in the congregation missing your most valuable points.

➢ Trying to demonstrate the audience is with you by frequently asking for an "Amen" is out of order. A better choice for involving the audience is encouraging them to "Give God a praise."

➢ You came to deliver a specific message; be certain you do that. Avoid expressing your personal opinions, telling jokes, or exposing grievances from the Pulpit. James (v.4) reminds us not to use slanderous words (whether it relates to persons or other denominations). This is particularly true during your delivery of The Word.

➢ Keep facing the congregation. Do not turn your back to the audience and preach to those behind you for an extended time.

➢ If you are the guest minister, get permission ahead of time to have special prayer or operate in the gifting of the Spirit. Yes, you are anointed and have the floor, but you must honor the angel of the house no matter what. God knows how to open any necessary door to accomplish His purposes, and the Spirit is HIGHLY intelligent!!

➢ Never accept an invitation to be a guest speaker without the permission of your pastor. If you have been invited to preach at another church by someone other than the pastor, make certain the host pastor has given his/her approval for your visit.

Your Posture

➢ Sit up straight. Do not fall asleep. Do not slump or lounge in your chair.

➤ Be alert and look alive. Women must always make certain their dresses provide adequate coverage, are long enough and have no revealing splits or dips while sitting or standing.

➤ When speaking, stand upright. Do not lean on the Pulpit. If you are somewhat nervous, you may be tempted to lean on the Pulpit. Nervousness is to be expected; rely upon God to see you through, and He will.

➤ The size of Pulpit areas will vary. Be observant and govern yourself accordingly. Endeavor to stay within an arm's reach of the Pulpit. Remain behind the Pulpit and on the Platform while you are delivering The Word. We do know that there are times when the Spirit takes the service in a different direction. At those times, we follow the Spirit's flow.

Come to the Pulpit Prepared.

➤ Come to the Pulpit prepared with what you need such as glasses, notes and your Bible. Many contemporary preachers use electronics devices as iPads, tablets, or cell phones. Practice using these tools correctly and efficiently. Be sure to turn off all the extra sound alerts. Despite using electronics, it is a good idea to bring your Bible to the Pulpit. This may avoid offending some congregants who may hold to "old fashioned" principles of reading from the Bible at the Pulpit.

➤ It is always wise to bring a hard copy of your sermon in case you need it (in case your device malfunctions). Knowing the audience to whom you will be speaking will help to ensure that your style and delivery technique are appropriate for the audience. Remember, "Let all things be done decently and in order."

➤ For your own comfort, bring a hand towel to the Pulpit with you. Do not use the same towel for blowing your nose and blotting perspiration.

Assisting in the Service.

Whoever is ministering is operating under the anointing at that time. Stand ready to assist the minister. Do only what the minister in charge may request of you, as you will then be operating under the same anointing. If the minister is already praying for someone, never go and begin praying for someone else unless you have been instructed to do so by the minister in charge. That is out of order and brings division, hindering the working of the Spirit.

If you are conducting Pulpit or have been asked to have closing remarks, have closing remarks and sit down or dismiss. Whatever you were asked to do, do that and no more, no less.

ORDER IN THE CHURCH

The Practice of Good Church Etiquette and Protocol
~ For the Ordained Deacon ~

The ordained deacon is subject to the same rules of conduct and comportment as the ordained minister. It follows, then, that the same rules of etiquette and protocol should be followed, whether at your local church or while visiting a different ministry. Although you do not customarily occupy a place on the Platform, as an ordained deacon (female, deaconess) you may sit on the Platform (in some denominations) if you are performing a specific part of the worship service. Your specific denomination or senior pastor will determine those guidelines.

The same guidelines regarding appropriate dress and Platform etiquette apply to you as you sit in the area reserved for ordained deacons in your local church or the church where you are a guest.

Visiting in an Official Capacity

➢ Deacons often have the privilege of visiting other churches in an official capacity ... meaning that you are there as a representative of the Diaconate of your local church. You may even be asked to represent your senior pastor at another church if one of the other ministers is not available. This is an honor and is usually the case for special ministry events such as anniversary celebrations.

➢ When you are visiting, you will follow the protocol established by that church. It is advisable, therefore, to inquire ahead of your visit, what will be expected of you. This information may be obtained from the Diaconate Chair of the church you are to visit. You will need to know, among other things: the time of the service, the dress code for the service, and your anticipated role on the program. If you are uncomfortable making this contact, your senior pastor should contact the pastor of the church and obtain the information for you. (**NOTE:** communication from Deacon to Deacon, Pastor to Pastor preserves order).

➢ We cannot place enough emphasis on the fact that all rules of order that the ordained minister is expected to follow apply to you as an ordained deacon. Do only what you have been called there to do and no more. If you are both an ordained deacon and a minister as well, do not attempt to demonstrate your ability to preach if you have been asked to have simple remarks as a member of the Diaconate.

It is important to state here that once you have been ordained as a deacon, you never lose that calling or position, even if you are elevated to Pulpit ministry. Remember that deacons and ministers are specialized servants. They all serve God by serving the people of God.

Visiting in an Unofficial Capacity

➢ When you have been given permission by your senior pastor to visit another church in an unofficial capacity (meaning you are not there as a representative of your local church's Diaconate or your pastor), you should always be cognizant of your comportment. Make a conscious effort to only engage in actions that will bring honor to God, your church, and your pastor.

➢ Many churches include a time to recognize guests during the worship service. If you are given an opportunity to stand and be recognized or give greetings, this can be done *"decently and in order"* as required by scripture (*I Corinthians 14:40*). A suggested response might be something like the following:

> "Good morning, with all honor and respect to God and the pastor of this congregation, my name is _____, and I am a member of _____Church. I greet you on behalf of my pastor, _____ and our congregation. I am grateful for the opportunity to fellowship with you today, and I have enjoyed the worship experience. Thank you, and God bless each of you."

THEN, TAKE YOUR SEAT!

➢ Familiarize yourself with the etiquette and protocol guidelines for ministers in the preceding section, and adopt those guidelines for your own conduct, from timeliness and following the directions of the Usher or Greeter, to the appropriate conduct you should adhere to in your seat.

APPENDICES

—

APPENDIX I
ORDINATION STAGES

Each denomination will have its own formalized Ordination Process for ensuring that Ordination candidates have been given the best possible preparation. In an effort to provide depth and structure for our own candidates, we developed the following set of stages.

STAGE I: Written Assignment
Focus: Introspection and Self-Assessment

DESCRIPTION

As you know, introspection involves taking an inward look at yourself from a natural and spiritual standpoint.

Self-assessment is your evaluation of your beliefs, actions and attitudes. In this paper, you will focus on your: skill sets, natural and spiritual self-awareness levels, and your fit for and commitment to Ministry. In preparing this assignment, include what you have learned about your:

> ➤ areas of strength
> ➤ areas in which you are deficient (areas that need work or growth)

Also include in your assignment:

> ➤ a clear statement of your belief about God
> ➤ a clear statement of what you believe about yourself

SUGGESTIONS TO HELP YOU THROUGH THIS PROCESS:

> Seek the face of God
> Ask God to reveal YOU to YOU (Be open with God. He already knows all there is to know about you anyway)
> Commit yourself to fasting and prayer as you never have before:

Fasting will help you gain increased control of your fleshly desires and actions.

ORDINATION STAGES

Fasting will help you become more sensitive to the Spirit of God and enable you to hear the voice of God even more clearly.

Although the following are customarily reserved for the ordained minister, ordained deacons would be wise to develop these skills, as they are often called upon to assist the minister in a number of these areas. In addition, many ministers often come from the ranks of the Diaconate.

STAGE II: Skills Demonstration
Focus: Your ability to effectively preside over/deliver various ministry events

DESCRIPTION

Demonstration of Ordinance and Ministry Event Competencies. In this stage you will perform the following before an audience of other ministers and/or members who will have an opportunity to provide constructive criticism/evaluation of your demonstration:

> Holy Communion
> Foot washing
> Baptism
> Weddings
> Funerals
> Christenings

Other ministry skills you will be asked to demonstrate relative to Pulpit protocol include:

> The Call to Worship
> Conducting the Service
> Scripture Reading (appropriateness for the occasion)
> Invocation
> Prayer of Comfort (funerals)
> Introduction of a Guest Preacher
> Invitation to Discipleship
> Altar Prayer
> Closing Remarks
> Benediction

ORDINATION STAGES

STAGE III: Skills Demonstration, Part I
Focus: Your ability to effectively preside over/deliver various ministry events

DESCRIPTION

This stage is a written exercise in two parts. Part I will allow you to demonstrate your ability in Platform/Pulpit protocol from the Call to Worship to the Benediction of a worship service.

You will prepare a 30-minute sermon script on one of the following using the KJV translation of the Bible, and deliver it as part of the service:

> John 1:1-3
> John 3:16
> Exodus 12 (Explain the significance of the blood on the doorposts)

STAGE III: Skills Demonstration, Part II
Focus: Your demonstration of biblical knowledge

DESCRIPTION

Part II will consist of a written response to 100 questions covering the following:

- ➤ Pentateuch (Genesis through Deuteronomy): 10 questions
- ➤ Historical Books (Joshua through Esther): 10 questions
- ➤ Books of Poetry (Job through Song of Solomon): 10 questions
- ➤ Major Prophets (Isaiah through Daniel): 10 questions
- ➤ Minor Prophets (Hosea through Malachi) 10 questions
- ➤ Biography (Matthew through John): 10 questions
- ➤ History (Acts) 10 questions
- ➤ Epistles (Romans-Jude) 10 questions
- ➤ Prophecy (Revelation) 10 questions
- ➤ Articles of Religion 10 questions

ORDINATION STAGES

STAGE IV: Interview with the Ordination Council
Focus: Your ability to effectively preside over/deliver various ministry events

DESCRIPTION

This interview is conducted by an Ordination Council (consisting of a committee of 3-5 experienced individuals from various levels of ministry), convened by your local pastor or ministry association). The Council's task is to evaluate your readiness for ordination in terms of your spiritual maturity and command of theological concepts.

Some denominations allow the candidate to select 1-2 persons to sit in on the Ordination Interview, although these individuals may or may not actively participate in the interview process. The areas to be addressed in the Interview include some or all, of the following. The list may indeed include other competency areas depending upon the denomination, in conjunction with the Council.

- ➤ The Candidate's Lifestyle and Personal Beliefs
- ➤ Worship and Sacraments
- ➤ Theological Competence
- ➤ Doctrinal Competence
- ➤ Church Polity (doctrine and organizational governance of the church)
- ➤ The Articles of Faith

APPENDIX II
SAMPLE ORDINATION INTERVIEW QUESTIONS

ORDINATION INTERVIEW QUESTIONS

The following represents a suggested set of categories and questions to be used in the Ordination Interview conducted by the Ordination Council. They are only suggestions and are not intended to be presented as "THE" set of questions to be asked of the candidates. Anyone desiring to utilize these questions may do so freely. Utilize them as they appear or in any order or format that best accommodates your specific denomination and/or purpose.

Ascertaining the lifestyle and character of the candidate: The following questions are intended to assist the council in gaining a personal perspective of the candidate. This is important because we believe that an individual's effectiveness in ministry will be significantly influenced by his/her character.

1. Describe what your normal, daily routine looks like.
2. The family unit was ordained by God. The quality and success of this unit will have an impact on your effectiveness in ministry. This question is two-fold. First, how would you rate the quality of your family life at the moment? Secondly, how do you make certain that the needs of your family are not neglected as you manage your ministry demands?
3. Name three major things you typically "juggle" during an average week. How is your time split between these things, and

how do you ensure that each area receives the proper amount of your attention?

4. What types of study aids do you most often use in preparing a sermon or Bible Study lesson?

5. Do you regularly build reading time into your week? What types of materials do you normally read? Briefly discuss one book you have read in the past month. Share the title, a summary of it, and what led you to read it.

6. For a myriad of reasons, scores of people struggle with credit and effective management of financial obligations. As a minister of the Gospel, do you feel it is important to maintain a good credit standing? Why or why not?

7. Are you faithful to your local church in the areas of supporting the mission and vision, tithing, and giving offerings, participating in the services and events, and in supporting your pastor?

Conversion

1. What is your understanding of the term conversion?
2. Give a brief account of Saul's conversion on the Damascus Road and compare that to your own Damascus Road experience.
3. What has changed in your life since you surrendered your life to God?
4. What major changes have taken place in your life since you answered the call to the ministry?

Ministry

1. Tell us about your call to the Word ministry. Include when and how you knew you were called, whether you immediately accepted and acknowledged the call, and what thoughts went through your mind at the time.

2. Accepting the call to ministry and deciding to obey God at all costs comes with a price to pay. Up to this point I am certain you have continued to experience attacks from the enemy simply because you are in the Kingdom of Light. Now you have some

added challenges because of the higher position you have taken. What have been some of those challenges you have faced, and how have you handled them?

3. What aspect of being a Pastor or Associate Pastor do you feel will give you the greatest degree of fulfillment or satisfaction?

4. In contemporary society, people typically lead very active lives. Tell us how you balance all you must do and yet have quality time for yourself.

5. Individuals in ministry often lead busier and more complicated lives than anyone else. Define burn-out in your terms and describe the plan you have in place to avoid falling victim to it.

6. Everyone needs to be accountable to someone, even Pastors. Do you have such an individual in your life? If so, who is that individual, and what is the process you use to evaluate your ministerial progress?

7. Describe the duties involved in pastoral care. Which do you like most, and why?

8. Which pastoral care duties do you like least and why?

9. Church administration is multi-faceted. Which aspects of church administration do you enjoy most and why?

10. Which aspect or aspects of church administration do you feel most confident or comfortable in?

11. If someone approached you on the street and asked you how he/she could be saved, what would you say? Include scripture references in your response.

12. Have you been given the opportunity to mentor another individual in ministry? Tell us how that come about, and why you feel your mentorship was successful.

13. Using a scale of 1 to 5, rate yourself as a preacher. Using that same scale, rate yourself as a teacher. Using that same scale, rate yourself as an overall minister, or servant leader. Knowing that none of us is perfect, what areas do you see yourself needing to improve in?

14. When is the last time you discussed your progress with your leader? What areas were indicated from your leader as needing improvement?

15. How long have you been a licensed minister in your church? What have you done to enhance the ministry of your church since being licensed?

BELIEFS
Personal Beliefs

1. How do you respond to people who ask, "How do I know I have been filled with the Holy Spirit"? Include scripture references.
2. The scriptures teach that, as ministers, we must live moral lives that are above reproach. Yet, the Apostle Paul declares in Romans 7:21 "When I would do good, evil is always present with me." How do you reconcile the two concepts?
3. Briefly describe your idea of what a church budget should look like. For example, what percentage of the total church budget should be devoted to personnel, to outreach, training, and any other areas you wish to share with.
4. Do you adhere to and actively support your church's Mission, Vision, Articles of Religion, Covenant, and general rules of operation?
5. What is your belief concerning what the Bible says about tithing and supporting the physical church with your personal resources?
6. Do you see tithing as a function of the modern-day church or do you see it as belonging to the Old Testament temple operations?
7. Knowing that Christ is soon to return, how does that fact influence your daily walk and ministry?
8. What is your understanding of ordination?

DOCTRINAL QUESTIONS
The Scriptures

1. Define the Holy Bible in your own words.
2. Describe the composition of the Bible.

3. Explain in your own words how the Bible was written.

4. What is the unifying theme of the Bible?

5. What makes you believe that the Bible is the authentic Word of God?

6. What is your understanding of what makes the Bible inerrant, and how does this fact impact your life and ministry?

7. We believe the Bible to be the ultimate authority in all situations. Do you also believe that, and if so, how does that fact guide your life and ministry?

8. Many people claim to preach the Gospel when they deliver the Word of God. What exactly is the Gospel?

9. What is the Fruit of the Spirit, and where can it be found in the Bible?

10. What are the Gifts of the Spirit, and where are they found in the Bible?

11. What are the Dispensations of the Bible and what eras do they cover?

12. What is your interpretation of works and the part they play in your salvation? Cite scripture references in your response.

The Godhead

1. In your own words, give us a summation of Genesis chapter 1. What do you identify as the most significant phrases in that chapter?

2. How is your personal salvation linked to the belief that God is the Creator?

3. The term trinity is not found in scripture. Yet, we believe in the Trinity. How is the doctrine of the Trinity presented in scripture? Give specific scriptural support for your response.

4. In John 10:10, Jesus gives a very brief, but thorough purpose for His coming to earth. He says: "The thief cometh not, but for to steal, and to kill, and to destroy: I am come that they might have life, and that they might have *it* more abundantly." What is His message here?

5. Most denominations or religious belief systems share many of the same core values. What is the major factor separating Christianity from most other major religious belief systems? Why is that significant to you?

6. Many contemporary religious factions teach that God is no longer performing miracles in the earth. How do you feel about that? Give scriptural support for your response, and any personal experience you may have had that has given rise to this response in you.

7. Share with us what you know of the attributes and nature of God. How does that knowledge affect your daily life and walk?

8. Briefly and in your own words, explain the virgin birth. Why was it essential to your salvation?

9. What is the significance of Jesus being our high priest and advocate with the Father?

10. What are Jesus' last words from the cross? Select one of them and discuss it in terms of its meaning and significance to your life and ministry.

11. Tell us your belief of how the Holy Spirit came to dwell with man. Can you relate that back to the book of Genesis, and Jesus' promise of a comforter?

12. What is the descriptive name for the Holy Ghost?

Man

1. Where in scripture can we find God's blueprint for the creation of man and the characteristics of the man he would create? How does that influence your life and ministry?

2. Briefly describe man's relationship with God at Creation.

3. Describe who and what Satan was in the beginning, and how did he become the fallen angel?

4. Give a brief account of man's fall from his relationship with God

5. Do you believe there is a specific God-ordained blueprint for each person's life?

6. Describe briefly the difference between the divine and the permissive will of God.

7. Why is it that men all too often operate in and live out the permissive will of God?

8. What was the significance of the animal sacrifices of the Old Testament?

Family

1. Although the Bible doesn't spend a great deal of time speaking specifically of the natural family structure, it is clearly in favor of that structure. How was the family unit implemented, and give scriptural references that indicate how the unit is to function.

2. Describe your personal belief about same-sex marriage and relationships. Can you support your belief with scripture?

3. The Bible states that a husband should love his wife as Christ loved the church. What is characteristic of that level of love? Is it achievable, and if so, how?

Salvation

1. Briefly describe what salvation is and the biblical process for being saved. Be as thorough as possible, making sure you include at least one scripture reference.

2. Explain briefly how the law was a shadow of good things to come, as stated in Hebrews 10:1.

3. Do you see any differences between salvation, justification, and sanctification? If so, what are those distinctions, and how are they achieved?

4. Why is it necessary for man to be sanctified?

5. Explain Romans 5:19 in your own words.

6. Some reformations teach that once an individual gives his life to Christ, he can never lose his salvation. Do you agree or disagree? Explain your answer.

The Church

1. What, in your view, was the original mission/purpose of the universal church? Do you believe that mission has changed since

the inception of the church? If so, what are those changes, and why has it changed?

2. How does an individual become a member of your local church?

3. Are you currently faithful to your local church body's services, events, teachings, and to its leadership?

4. Share your understanding of the church as the Body of Christ vs. the Bride of Christ.

5. In contemporary society, some believe it is not necessary to attend a church or gather and fellowship with other believers. Is this belief supported by the Word of God? Give a scriptural reference for your response.

Ordinances of the Church

1. Give the definition of an Ordinance. What are the Ordinances of the Church?

2. Where in scripture did each of the Ordinance originate?

3. Define baptism. Do you believe it is necessary for believers to be baptized? Why or why not?

4. How does baptism relate to Christ's sacrifice, and what does baptism indicate to the outside world, family and friends?

5. Describe the sacraments of the Lord's Supper (Holy Communion) and what these sacraments represent. How do you know what they represent?

6. Should every believer participate in Holy Communion? Why or why not?

7. How is participating in Holy Communion beneficial to the believer? Can it also be detrimental to an individual? How do you know?

8. When Jesus washed the disciples' feet, it was not really necessary for Him to do so. Why not? Why, then, did He do so?

9. Many believe today that foot washing is not one of the ordinances. What are your thoughts on this, and do you believe we should observe the practice of foot washing? Why or why not?

10. Are there any other ways of demonstrating the spirit of foot washing in contemporary society?

Evangelism and Missions

1. State where "The Great Commission" is found in the Bible, and briefly explain its significance for that time and contemporary society.
2. In what ways do you believe your ordination will enable you to engage more fully in the evangelism and missions efforts of your local church body?
3. Do you know how your local church body is engaged in missions?

Service and Stewardship

1. Give a brief, but thorough description of what stewardship is, and explain what it means to your life personally.
2. What is meant by the tithe?
3. Some dismiss tithing as a forced action under the "Law." What do you believe about tithing as a part of the Christian's responsibility to God?
4. Are you now and will you continue to be a role model of tithing to your local church body?
5. The Bible teaches us to tithe our resources to the local church so they may be utilized to advance the Kingdom of God on earth and enhance the work of the local ministry. Do you also see your time as a resource that can be tithed for these purposes?
6. What is the meaning of "Deacon", and who were the first Deacons?
7. What is the role of the Deacon in the modern-day church?
8. Where are Deacons described in scripture?
9. How can the Pastor, Governing Board, Ministry Departments and Congregants function together to provide effective ministry to the community?
10. Describe what you see as Pastoral Counseling.

The Five-Fold Ministry

1. Define the Five-Fold Ministry. Briefly describe the operational level of each office.

2. What is another name for the Five-Fold Ministry and why is it called this?

3. What was the purpose behind Christ implementing the Five-Fold Ministry?

The Candidate's Relationship to the Local Church

1. Explain how the church body can be both independent and cooperative. Give some specific examples citing your own local church congregation.

2. Explain your understanding of what is meant by the term "servant-leader."

3. Are you ready to fully serve your local church in the role of "servant-leader?" Are there any areas or duties that may be a challenge for you?

4. Are you now, and will you continue to be exemplary in adhering to the Constitution and By-laws of your local church?

5. Discuss the meaning of Hebrews 13:7 "Obey them that have the rule over you …"

The End of all Things

1. The term rapture is not found in scripture. Give the definition of this word. Do you believe it is a physical, visible event that will take place? Give scriptural reference(s) in your response.

2. What is your understanding of the tribulation period?

3. What is your understanding of the millennial reign?

4. Briefly describe what happens in Revelation, chapter 20.

5. What is the definition of eschatology? What does this term have to do with the blessed hope?

6. As God's people, what should we be doing in preparation for the second coming of the Lord?

7. What happens to people when they die … both saved and unsaved?

8. What will be the fate of unbelievers? What will happen to believers? Do you have scripture to support your answers?

9. How do you interpret II Corinthians 5:10?
10. Do you believe that Heaven and hell are both real places?
11. What do the scriptures teach about heaven and hell?
12. How do you interpret "a new heaven and a new earth?"
13. We believe we are currently living in the Dispensation of Grace. What does that mean to you?

AFTERWORD

It is a blessing in such a time as this to be afforded the privilege to have this great book, that is timely, necessary, and ordained of God. I am honored to share in this moment in time. I will definitely purchase copies as a refresher course for myself and to use in further advancing the edification of God's people.

Sincerely,

In His Service
Overseer Gregory Blocker

Deliverance Has Come Ministries, Inc.
Newark, New Jersey

Printed in the United States
by Baker & Taylor Publisher Services